CISTERCIAN STUDIES SERIES: NUMBER TWENTY-SEVEN

THOMAS MERTON

CISTERCIAN STUDIES SERIES

Board of Editors

CISTERCIAN STUDIES SERIES: NUMBER TWENTY-SEVEN

Thomas Merton

The Man and His Work

Dennis Q. McInerny

CISTERCIAN PUBLICATIONS
CONSORTIUM PRESS
Washington, D.C.
1974

Cistercian Studies Series   ISBN 0-87907-800-6
This Volume   ISBN 0-87907-827-8

Library of Congress Catalog Card Number 74-4319

IN MEMORIAM
Roger J. McInerny, Jr.
1950 - 1970

CONTENTS

INTRODUCTION

T HIS IS A BOOK ABOUT THOMAS MERTON, an attempt to put between two covers the marrow of the man and his thought. It makes no pretensions to being a definitive work. Apart from the possibility that a definitive work on Thomas Merton might be a contradiction in terms, my intention was not so much to say the last word as to provide a fitting and reliable beginning for anyone interested in becoming acquainted with an extraordinary monk. Though intended for the general reader rather than the scholar, I would hope that a scholar could read the book with some enjoyment and perhaps even a little benefit.

Merton was an intriguing man, and for that reason it is easy to write about him—perhaps too easy. The danger is that, because he was so many-sided, because he appeals to a diversity of people for a diversity of reasons, one is apt to select only those things which titillate one's own fancies or biases and ignore the rest; and the end result is a distorted picture. He was a complicated man. That in itself is scarcely a claim to fame; the world is full of complicated men. The difference with Merton is that he was complicated in interesting ways. One of the chief aims of this study is to capture the complexity of Thomas Merton, to view him from as many sides as possible in the hope that all those views taken together would add up to a picture of him which is at once full and faithful.

No reader will have to read very far before discovering that this is in the main an admiring book. I like Thomas Merton.

But this is not an exercise in unmitigated praise. My approach is critical; I have set down here both my positive and negative estimates of his life and his work. If I had neglected the negative while accentuating the positive, the product would have been irresponsible and unbelievable. The Merton I would have ended up with would have been a caricature. The most vociferous complainer against such a caricature would have been Merton himself, who had a very low tolerance for the obnoxious artificiality of rosey-cheeked, plaster of Paris sanctity.

ACKNOWLEDGEMENTS

Very few books are the product of one person alone, and this book is no exception. Professor Mulford Q. Sibley of the University of Minnesota was the first to encourage me to write on Merton, and while preparing this book I continued to profit from the able direction he gave me. In one degree or another, the influence of many people at Minnesota is to be found in this book, notably that of Professors Mary C. Turpie, David W. Noble and Joseph J. Kwiat. And my thanks are due to several librarians there, most of them nameless, who made my research not only less painful but at times even pleasurable. I must also thank, for their kindness and help, the librarians at the College of St. Thomas and at the Merton Room of Bellarmine-Ursuline College.

Sister M. Therese Lentfochr, sds, a close friend of Thomas Merton, and, like him, a poet, was most generous in giving me full access to the varied and rich selection of material she has in her possession. Of special value was the original manuscript of *The Seven Storey Mountain*, from which I quote in this book. Thomas Merton himself was not to be outdone in generosity, responding to my queries promptly and frankly and sending me material, much of it unpublished, which I otherwise would not have known about. Since Father Merton's death, Brother Patrick Hart, ocso, his secretary, has gone out of his way to be of help. He has read and commented upon my dissertation, graciously submitted to private conferences wherein we discussed Merton at length, and—most important of all—read and commented upon the manuscript for this book. For all of which I am deeply grateful. My colleagues in the English department at Bradley Unversity have provided constant stimulus, directly and indirectly, for my thought on Merton, and to the University itself I wish to express appreciation for being given a summer off to develop this book. The Committee on Faculty Research and Creative Production provided me with a grant to cover the cost of typing the manuscript.

I owe a great deal to the wide reading in secondary materials I have done over the past five years. Among books on Merton which I have enjoyed and learned from are John Howard Griffin's *A Hidden Wholeness*, Edward Rice's *The Man in the Sycamore Tree*, James Thomas Baker's *Thomas Merton Social Critic*, and John J. Higgin's *Merton's Theology of Prayer*. If it would not be too eccentric to do so, I would like to acknowledge all the contributors to this book of whom I am either forgetful or unconscious. Finally, while I thank all of these people I wish to embarrass none of them. The flaws of the book are entirely my own.

CHAPTER I

A LIFE

WE TOO OFTEN MAKE THE MISTAKE, when we get interested in the ideas of a man, of separating his intellectual life from his total life. A thinker formulates his ideas and wrestles them to paper, not in a vacuum, but in context, within the framework of daily duties, often in the face of distractions, and sometimes while laboring under the weight of disappointments and discouragements. Understanding that context can contribute measurably to a better understanding of the ideas which emanated from it. It would be foolish to argue that one cannot hope to grasp Thomas Merton's thought without a thorough knowledge of the circumstances of his life, but it would be equally foolish carelessly to underrate the real values which such a knowledge can provide, foremost among which would be a deeper and richer comprehension of Merton's thought. Too, knowledge of biography helps us maintain a sense of perspective, reminding us that in all circumstances we are dealing here with a man, a human being, and not a bloodless abstraction whom we have conveniently labeled a "thinker".

The best provider thus far of biographical material on Thomas Merton has been Thomas Merton. He has written a great deal about himself. The best source is certainly *The Seven Storey Mountain*, a book which recounts his story from birth to his thirty-third year. It is the proper place to begin for anyone who wants to become acquainted with Merton, and it is must reading for anyone who wants to take

1

him seriously. Other books which contain valuable biographical information are *The Sign of Jonas* (1956) and *The Secular Journal* (1959).

He was born in France in 1915, in a small town tucked away in the Pyrenees called Prades. His mother, Ruth Jenkins, was an American, the child of a Long Island couple who had loose alliances with the Quakers and strong feelings for pacifism. His father Owen was a New Zealander and a painter. It was while he was studying art in Paris that he had met his wife; she also had aspirations to be an artist at the time. Perhaps one of the unconscious promptings which eventually led Thomas Merton to take a vow of stability in a monastic order was the intensely peripatetic nature of his early life. He was about a year old when his parents brought him to this country, primarily on account of the intrusion of World War One, secondarily because Owen Merton's parents-in-law opposed his desire to enter that war. The next few years were spent in the United States. During that time his brother John-Paul was born, four years younger than himself, and during that time also he commenced his formal education in the local public school.

When he was six years old his mother died of cancer. A strangely strong woman—she seems somehow all the more vivid for the little we know about her—she apparently decided that it would be harmful for her children to see her in her decaying and dying state, so once she was hospitalized as a terminal patient she would not allow them to be brought to her. Shortly before her death she wrote young Thomas a letter, in which she explained that he would never see her again. For someone his age, it must have been a very disconcerting message about a very disconcerting subject. After the death of his mother, Merton was taken by his father to Bermuda, where they remained a few months while the father painted and the son continued his education on a very sporadic basis. Then it was back to Long Island to live with his maternal grandparents and John-Paul while his father went off to Europe.

When Thomas was ten, in 1925, his father brought him to Europe to live with him. They settled down in Montauban, a town in the south of France and Thomas was enrolled in the nearby Lycée Ingres. After two years there he was sent to England, where he attended first Ripley Court School in Surrey and then Oakham School in the Midlands. It was from Oakham that he matriculated to Clare College, Cambridge, in the fall of 1933, having been awarded an exhibition to read modern languages. The one year he spent at Cambridge was by every account that Merton gives a decidedly unpleasant one. He obviously had no great love for the place, and spent more time raising cane and socializing than he did studying. None the less, he did pass his tripos in modern languages at the end of the year, with a Second, and was planning to return to the University the following fall, which is to say the fall of 1934. At the suggestion of his godfather, a London physician who was acting as his guardian, he had formulated the vague intention of entering the British diplomatic service after getting his degree. Displeased with his dissipation at Cambridge, however, his guardian recommended that he give up the idea and go to live with his grandparents in America. There was really nothing to keep him in Europe now, for his father had died a few years previously, a slow, agonizing death of a tumor on the brain.

So, it was in December 1934 that the young Merton came to live permanently in the United States. He had been reading heavily in Marx at the time and he conceived of himself as a communist. Having decided that study of literature and the arts was hopelessly bourgeois and socially useless, his intention was to enroll in the New School of Social Research once he arrived in New York. What he actually did was enroll at Columbia, where in the spirit of his initial resolve he first concentrated on the social sciences but eventually—in great part due to the influence of Mark Van Doren—abandoned his temporary and not altogether convincing antipathy for literature and became an English major. Merton was in every way a Big Man on the Columbia campus. A tireless activist, if there was anything to get involved in he got involved in it. He was a fraternity man. He was on the track team, until his heavy smoking, steady drinking and minimal sleeping eventually forced him to sever his ties with not only track but with all collegiate athletics. He wrote, and profusely, for every campus publication; in his senior year he became editor-in-chief of the year book, *The Columbian*, and art editor of the *Jester*, a campus literary magazine. The intense social concern he brought with him to Columbia was manifested by his membership in the National Students' League. For a time, until the incongruity of the meetings being held in plush Park Avenue apartments proved too much for even his capacity for the paradoxical, he was a card-carrying member of the Communist Party. He even had a party name: Frank Swift. For all his extra-curricular activity, though, Merton found time to give more than perfunctory attention to his studies. He developed a deep love for and incisive understanding of literature. He took his B.A. in 1938 and his M.A. a year later. His master's thesis was written on a poet who was going to continue to influence him for the rest of his life, William Blake. He had begun work on his doctorate, with the plan to write the dissertation on Gerard Manley Hopkins, when an event transpired which was to alter radically the whole course of his life.

That event was his conversion to Catholicism in 1938. Despite the manner in which he plays up the errant "paganism" of his youth, Merton was throughout his life an essentially religious person, which is to say that he was always possessed of an irrepressible sense of wonder at and passion for ultimate reality. In Catholicism he found a home where both his vibrant intellectual curiosity and wide-ranging mystical tendencies could live at peace and be assuaged. It was not long after his conversion that he began seriously to think of becoming a priest. He applied for admission to the Franciscan order, was accepted, and was on the verge of entering their novitiate when he was overpowered by a sense of unworthiness after reviewing the escapades of his past life. He explained his qualms to the Franciscans and they suggested that he put off entering the novitiate, perhaps indefinitely. Merton was crushed, but he accepted the decision with courage, deciding that if he could not live in a monastery he would live as a monk in the world. Among other observances he scheduled for himself, he prayed the full Divine Office every day just as if he were ordained. Since his conversion Merton had been teaching English at the Extension Division of Columbia University and, later, at St. Bonaventure's University in Olean, New York. It was while he was at St. Bonaventure's that he met Catherine de Hueck, who had recently established a settlement house in Harlem. He seriously considered leaving teaching to go to work with her there. As it happened, he did leave teaching, in December 1941, not to go to Harlem but to become a Trappist monk.

Merton had first heard of the Trappists from Daniel Walsh, a man from whom he had taken a course in scholastic philosophy at Columbia and who is himself now a priest. At Father Walsh's suggestion, he journeyed to the Trappist monastery in Kentucky to make a retreat. It was a matter of love at first sight. Harsh and secluded though it was, Merton saw in the life of the Cistercians of the Strict Observance the life he wanted to lead. Back in Olean he made quick preparations to wrap up his worldly affairs. St. Bonaventure agreed to get someone to take his courses so he could leave in mid-year. Registered with his draft board as a Noncombatant Objector, he wrote to them and requested that they delay his induction pending his possible acceptance by the Trappists. Then, holding his breath, fearing that they might find in him the same objections which disconcerted the Franciscans, he wrote to the Trappists and asked permission to join their order. They told him to come.

On December 10, 1941, three days after the bombing of Pearl Harbor, he passed through the gates of the Abbey of Gethsemani near Bardstown, Kentucky. After Merton entered the monastery there were very few "events"—other than the death of his brother John-Paul, killed in action in 1943, and perhaps the publication of his books—which marked his life, which is precisely how he intended it to be.

A man becomes a monk not to do things but to become someone, and becoming someone is not announced by superficial eventfulness. In 1947 he made his solemn vows, which is to say he committed himself to the monastic life for good. Two years later he was ordained a priest. In 1951 he became an American citizen, a step which he was prompted to take, he explained later, because of his admiration for Emily Dickinson and Henry David Thoreau. If it was all right for them it was all right for him. For four years he served as the Master of Scholastics, the director and counselor of those monks who are studying for ordination. Then, in 1955, he was appointed to the position of Master of Novices, one of the most critical posts in any religious order. It is the duty of the Master of Novices to introduce the newcomers to the monastic life, and to make the difficult and touchy decision of who should and should not stay on. He held this post until 1965 when, after many years of effort, he obtained permission from his abbot to live the life of a hermit. Aided by fellow monks, and a local contractor, he built a small hermitage in a wooded area about a mile from the main buildings and it was there he spent most of the remaining three years of his life.

The greatest recognition which Thomas Merton received during his lifetime was in the large number of people who read his works and were impressed and guided by his thought. But there were also more specific forms of recognition. In 1961 Columbia University named him a recipient of the Medal of Excellence, given to distinguished graduates. In 1963 he was awarded the Pax Medal by the Massachusetts Political Action for Peace for his antiwar writings, and also in 1963 the University of Kentucky conferred upon him an honorary Doctor of Laws degree.

Once Merton entered the monastery he very rarely left it, and seldom did he travel further than Louisville, fifty miles away. It was all the more unusual, then, that he embarked in the fall of 1968 on an extensive trip to the Far East. The length of his stay was undetermined. He had been asked to come to the Far East by various Trappist abbots, first, to attend a conference on monasticism to be held in Bangkok in December, second, to visit several Trappist monasteries in the orient in the capacity of a consultant and advisor. It was anticipated that he could stay at any one of these monasteries for several months. Before going to Bangkok he traveled extensively in India, where he met and talked with the Dalai Lama. At the conference in Bangkok he gave in the morning an informal talk on the relationships between Marxism and monasticism. He was scheduled to return that afternoon for a panel discussion on the subject, but he never did. Around 4 p.m. he was found dead in his room. Though the fact that he died alone makes it impossible to establish beyond the shadow of a doubt the exact cause of death, all indications seem to point to the conclusion that he was killed accidentally, electrocuted by a defective electric fan. It was December 10, 1968, twenty-seven years to the day since he had entered the monastery. He was fifty-three years old.

CHAPTER II

"BEHOLD, YOU WILL BE SILENT "

WHEN THOMAS MERTON ENTERED a Trappist monastery in December of 1941 he embarked upon a life which cut him off from normal concourse with the American public. Unlike contemporaries of comparable prestige and celebrity, he was not exposed to the steady diet of newspaper, magazine, radio and television interviews by which our society regularly attempts to explore every nook and cranny of its men of letters to see what makes them tick. Neither did he ever go on the college lecture tour, to read his poetry or express his views, and later to field questions from a querulous audience, and later still to try to cope with the oppressive clubbiness at the cocktail party in the home of a concerned professor. That Merton was spared these dubious delights was unquestionably to his benefit, but it leaves us without sources of information about him which may have been valuable. All this is by way of emphasizing the fact that Merton's main means of communicating with the world was through his own writing. Because so much of his life was dedicated to writing, because to talk about Merton the writer is to talk about a very crucial part of his total identity, because, again, so much of his person and virtually all of his ideas were transmitted to us through his writing, it makes good sense to begin this study proper by discussing Merton the writer.

The title of this chapter is ironic. The words, "behold, you will be silent," played a significant part in Merton's life. In *The Seven Storey Mountain* he tells us about the occasion when, while teaching at St. Bonaventure's, unsure whether or not it was his destiny to be a Trappist, he resorted—somewhat hesitantly it should be noted—to the remedy of opening the Bible at random and putting his finger blindly on a passage to see what answer it might provide. His eyes fell upon *"ecce eris tacens,"* the words spoken by the angel to Zachary, the father of John the Baptist. Though he was later to feel somewhat sheepish about this action, fearing that it smacked dangerously of superstition, the words did set him back on his heels at the time. "Behold you will be silent." Was it coincidence or providence which impregnated these words with their special significance for him? He was thinking seriously about becoming a Trappist, of living a life of obscurity and silence. The Bible seemed to say that it would be so.

But insofar as that incident was prophetic in its implications, it was ambivalently so. True, Merton did join the Trappists; he did join an order which is chiefly known by the fact that its members abide by a strict rule of silence—indeed, if people know nothing else about the Trappists they know this about them. But did Merton lead a life of silence? Hardly. Speaking is not the only way of breaking silence; writing also does the job, and judging from the amount which Merton wrote he has to be regarded as anything but a man of silence. To the contrary, he is one of the most talkative Trappists on record.

This is one of the major ironies of Thomas Merton's story. Here is a man who made a dramatic decision radically to alter the course of his life. He determined to give up the world, to turn his back on all previously conceived notions of what he should be and what he should do. Among such notions was the idea of being a writer, specifically a novelist. His decision made, that idea was now seen as straw, a feeble vanity which had been nourished by his pagan pride. Writing was—at least for him—a wordly occupation, a distraction. He wanted to put it behind, to live for God alone. His name was now Frater Louis. He wanted "Thomas Merton" to shut up, to remain a person of the past. He wanted simply to fade away without frenetics or fanfare, to lead the silent life. So he took what one would suppose to have been a remarkably logical step to fulfill this desire: he entered a Trappist monastery. And what happened? He became a world famous author. "Thomas Merton" not only refused to be muzzled, he gained heights of pre-eminence which, in all likelihood, he never would have gained had he stayed back in New York and followed through on his earlier plans to be an academic or a novelist.

It is odd how many people want to hold Merton personally at fault for this bizarre turn of events, as if he had deliberately planned it this way. More than once I have heard Catholics complain about this prolific monk who belonged to an order which was supposedly bound to silence, as if with every publication he was betraying a sacred trust. But non-Catholics as well seem to be offended by the incongruity, not so much for ethical reasons, but rather because they feel that there are in the circumstance overtones of aesthetic impropriety. Trappists simply should not write that much; it is not the way things are supposed to be. These reactions aside, it is important to know that Merton's becoming very much the complete writer, and in the process losing out on the privacy and silence he came to the monastery to find, was not altogether the result of his own choice.

Whatever residual longings to be a writer, particularly a poet, may still have been clinging to his unconscious when he came to the monastery, it is abundantly evident that he had definitely decided to give up writing once he arrived. He did not reach this decision without a considerable amount of difficulty, perhaps even pain, for Merton—if such phrases mean anything at all—was a natural writer. Writing was in his blood, and he put words to paper as much out of need as desire. For him, as for many writers of the same cut (Thoreau and Wolfe, for example), the act of writing was a way of realizing the world, of bringing to term events, thoughts, emotions—the various and disparate stuff of any person's existence—which otherwise would have remained in a permanently embryonic state within his mind. And yet, though writing lay close to the center of his being—perhaps *because* it did—he saw it as an impediment rather than an aid to the task which must now demand all of his dedication and energies. The original manuscript of *The Seven Storey Mountain* contains several passages which did not appear in the published version and which tellingly recount the struggle he was going through at this time.

It seems that for a while after his arrival at the monastery Merton continued to keep a journal, and perhaps work out a poem every now and then. But he quickly brought himself up short on this matter. The manuscript states: "I used to be a writer, but God wants me to die to all that. I shall give up all writing. Nothing more, not even a spiritual journal. Poems I renounce forever: did I come to the monastery to be a poet? God forbid." That seems unambiguous enough. Apparently, however, no doubt in the conviction that he was at fault for doing so, Merton mentioned to his confessor that he had been writing poems. Instead of being admonished by him he was encouraged. He was told that writing poems can be a form of prayer. But he was hesitant to agree, and rather than this assurance settling his mind it only caused him the more consternation. He then went to the abbot, not so much to get further advice, but simply to have the superior of the monastery override the decision of his confessor. But the abbot thought that the confessor's advice was sound, and told Frater Louis to continue writing. He tried to impress upon him that writing should be considered by him as his monastic work; while others made cheese or washed clothes or sculpted statues or plowed fields, Frater Louis would write books. The young monk did not find the prospect encouraging, and not to be easily put off in his determination to quit writing altogether, he even went so far as to ask the Abbot General of the Cistercians, during his visitation at Gethsemani, if he would give him permission to cease and desist once and for all. The Abbot General said no. He told Merton that he should write in a spirit of peace and equanimity; he could never go totally wrong by obeying his superiors.

Merton did obey, but not without, one imagines, heaving a

deep sigh of resignation. It was as if he had been driven to give up writing by an instinctive notion of what was right for him to do. If he could not now give it up he would at least completely transform it. It would become something entirely different than it had hitherto been for him. He would write now no longer for Thomas Merton but for God. But it was not going to be easy. In fact, he was convinced that by being saddled with the obligation to write, and willingly accepting that obligation in the spirit of obedience, he had taken on one of the most formidable crosses which it would be his duty to bear as a Cistercian monk. Thus, in a relatively short span of time, things had come full circle with regards to Merton's plans for his writing. He sums up the situation for us in the original manuscript for *The Seven Storey Mountain.* "So in the end, after a lot of twisting and turning and scruples and questions I am still what I started out to be in the beginning: I am still a writer."

He certainly was, and in years to come he was going to turn into a writer the likes of which, I am sure, he had no conception of when he wrote those lines. But knowing what we do know about the circumstances which led to Merton's developing into one of the most prolific Trappists in history, I think we should be slow to find in this eventuality reasons for casting aspersions upon him. He was not so much disloyal to Trappist silence as he was loyal to Trappist obedience. And to obey, especially in matters which were difficult and in which your own instincts were urging you in the opposite direction, was for him to act virtuously; further, the act of obedience, far from being debilitatingly deferential or even slavish, was (and Teilhard de Chardin saw this as well) an eminently free and freeing act of love. We find this attitude difficult if not impossible to understand, we who are so obsessed with freedom that in the mad pursuit of it we have passed it by—in the meantime becoming hopelessly entangled and inhibited in our own complex and convoluted concepts.

Why, we might ask, did Merton make such a fuss over continuing his writing once he entered the monastery? Understood, he wanted seriously and uncompromisingly to seek perfection, to become a saint, and this, he determined, would be a full time job. But surely he was well aware that many great saints—Thomas Aquinas, Bonaventure, Teresa of Avila, John of the Cross—combined writing with the seeking of sanctity. Indeed he was aware of these precedents, read them and admired them, but also had the honesty and perspicacity to see that he differed substantially from these saints, that the peculiarities of his temperament were such as to make writing for him a special problem and a special burden, a hindrance to sanctity rather than a help to it. The problem was not uniquely his, but seems to be part and parcel of a modern idea of the writer and the way he should look upon life with which Merton was imbued as he was coming of age and according to which, in his apprentice years—back in the days when he won Columbia's "best writer of the year award" and later when he was turning out novels à la Hemingway—he was trying to live.

According to this idea the writer is a kind of Prometheus, a god-defying individualist who by main force wrests from the niggardly powers that be the divine fires of inspiration. So often the modern writer (and when I say "modern" I mean to encompass the past 130 years or so), especially the American, is one in a constant cramp over himself and his art. He does not so much live life as fight it. He is most assured of his being alive, of his being aware as an artist, if he is agonizing and suffering. Ostensibly the writer writes about his world, about people who surround him and events of which he has either proximate or remote acquaintance, but in fact he is writing primarily about himself. His works are just so many projections of his inner and often pitifully limited world, so many tedious variations on the theme of ego-as-god. Apart from the anemic results following upon this distorted conception of the literary artist and literary artistry, it also carries with it no small dangers for the writer himself, and, as is to be expected, he is the one who is often the first to discover this. Nathaniel Hawthorne, for example, was well aware of the perils of taking what might be called a centripetal rather than a centrifugal view of art, the chief being that soon you become a mere observer of life rather than a liver of it. And though this is bad enough, from this plane you can degenerate further, into being a manipulator of other people—in fact or in imagination no matter; the dire psychological consequences for the writer are the same either way.

Merton realized that the kind of soul-searching that a writer often engages in is going to have confining rather than liberating consequences. He burrows into his psyche not to break through into a world infinitely large and wondrous, but simply to build a musty little lair, littered with the debris of his hacked-at life, in which he can snuggle up to his shivering artist Self and derive from it what meagre warmth his imagination will allow. Too often the inwardness of the writer leads to nothing but a dead-end, and this was precisely the kind of inwardness—a false inwardness, if you will—that Merton wanted to get away from. The meditative experiences he associated with writing were unpleasant and, in the deepest sense, unproductive—desperate exercises of the spiritually impotent, efforts to flee from life rather than confront it directly. It is little wonder, then, that he was so adamant in wanting to chuck the writing overboard. With his becoming a monk he had dedicated himself to an entirely different brand of inwardness than that with which he had been familiar up to that time; the idea now was to plumb the depths in order to expand one's world, not shrink it, to break through the pressing parameters of Self and discover the boundless reality of God. His experiences with writing had been overly one-sided, revolving too much around the idea of the writer as obsessed ego-centric, of writing as the product of a weary routine of dedicated navel-gazing. He was to discover that the world of art was much wider than he had initially conceived it, that a writer, writing, is open to other interpretations. Specifically, he was to learn that writing could truly qualify as monastic work, that is, that it could be a help rather than a hindrance along the road to perfection. This is not to say that it suddenly ceased to be a bother and a distraction to him, for it did not—in fact it was throughout his life the cross which he said it was going to be—but at least he overcame the idea that there was something intrinsically evil for him in being a writer. There was, after all, a place in the monastery for "Thomas Merton," and despite their sometime differences, he and Frater Louis would just have to learn to get along together.

Once he overcame his initial scruples about writing, he entered into it with gusto. He was not one to do things by half-measures, and few modern writers can match his prolific output. He had begun writing before he entered the monastery, as we saw, producing a lot of material for student publications at Columbia and while in graduate school doing book reviews for the New York *Times* as well as the *Herald Tribune*. He also wrote four and a half novels; three and a half of which he burned before coming to Gethsemani, the remainder, which he had called *The Journal of My Escape from the Nazis* and which he brought along with him, was published posthumously (1969) as *My Argument with the Gestapo*. But it was not until after he had been living as a monk for about five years that he began writing in earnest, that is, at such a pace as to make this early productivity pale by comparison. He kept up this breath-taking pace, perhaps even increasing it gradually, for the remaining twenty or so years of his life. By the time of his death in 1968 he had authored over fifty published books, besides literally dozens of separate articles, poems, prefaces and miscellany. But his published works represent only a part of his total out put. He wrote many things which were promulgated in a limited way only, run off on a mimeograph machine and distributed either just to his students at Gethsemani or to selected Cistercian and Benedictine monks in monasteries around the country. Finally, much of his material was not made public in any way, but we can look forward to its being published in the future. It has been estimated that new Merton material, much of which will require extensive editing, will be appearing on the market at a more or less steady rate for the next twenty-five years.

Merton wrote a lot. Did he perhaps write too much? Was he, in his desire to do his monastic work with uncompromising devotion perhaps somewhat over-zealous? I bring up the question only because he did, and he answered it in the affirmative. Many of his friends shared that opinion, and one suggested that Merton, simply as a matter of policy, should burn every third thing that he wrote. Having read all of his published works and a great many of the unpublished ones, I too would agree that he wrote too much. But what does it mean to say that a writer has written too much? Certainly it is not to fault him for being prolific, to claim that there is something wrong with quantity as such; rather, on the other hand, it is to make the point that quality has suffered on account of quantity. He tried to get too many things out too fast. The most noticeable effects of this in his writing were a high degree of repetitiousness, poor organization (especially of shorter pieces), and carelessly developed or underdeveloped ideas.

One explanation for his precipitousness in letting things go which were not really ready for publication was his inability to say no. Once he become famous as a writer, once, that is, his name became calculable in terms of dollars and cents, he was prevailed upon by many editors, especially of Catholic magazines, to submit pieces for publication, often on subjects of considerable complexity, which, to have been done in the best possible way, would have required much more time and research than he was able to give them. And there were the many authors who asked him to do prefaces for their books. And there were the many worthy causes which asked for statements and short essays for their news-letters or little magazines. He tried to honor every request—at least up to the point, in the late sixties, when the whole thing began to get out of hand—with the inevitable result that not a few of the pieces which appeared under his name were not worthy of it. In writing, as in everything else, you can only spread yourself so thin.

But we cannot entirely blame outside sources for the diminution of quality resulting from an overemphasis upon quantity. Merton himself, at least with respect to style, often took a casual attitude toward writing. He could never be

accused of being a stylist, if we mean by that one who agon-
izes over the *mot juste*, one who tinkers with a phrase until
its ring is true and polishes it until it shines. He liked to get
things done, and once they were done to move on to something else. This we have by his own admission. If the piece
just finished was somewhat less than perfect, well, no matter;
he could not dawdle over it. There was more writing that lay
ahead. It was not uncommon, as his agent and editor Naomi
Burton has told us, for him to send off to a publisher a manuscript for a book which was so hastily put together and
haphazardly edited that two of its chapters were virtually
identical in content. I said he took a casual attitude toward
writing with respect to style, but not toward writing as such.
Writing he took very seriously, not as a way of displaying
one's verbal finesse but principally as a means of communication. For Merton, what he had to say was always more
important than how he said it, and if he often rushed into
print it was because he sincerely felt he had something to say.

What Merton had to say was said in an amazing number of
different areas. His first published book was a volume of poetry, and over the course of his life he was to publish seven
more. We then can confidently describe him as a poet—the
way, incidentally in which he preferred to be described. But
the description is limited, for poetry is only a small part of
his writing story. He also wrote hagiography, biography,
autobiography, history, philosophy, theology, social criticism, literary criticism, fiction and meditations. In practically
everything, he wrote primarily as an amateur, or, to put it
another way, as an essayist. Merton neither pretended to be
nor wanted to be an expert in most of the fields in which he
worked. His primary intent was to explore, to discover, to try
out his ideas. He wrote about things he was interested in;
specialization or the lack thereof was not the kind of matter
he worried over. It would not be overstating the case to say
that he was motivated by the Renaissance idea that no part
of the world of knowledge was closed to the lively and in-
quiring mind. A cursory glance at the Merton canon reveals
that relatively few of his works are books strictly speaking,

that is, lengthy organic treatments of a single subject. Among such are *The Seven Storey Mountain, The Waters of Siloe* and *The Ascent to Truth*. By far the greater number of his prose works are journals, collections of meditations (which vary in the degree of their organic coherence), and collections of essays—the products of a man who used writing as much as a means of learning as a means of teaching. He wrote to provide answers, it is true, but also to find out what were the proper questions.

Although many writers like to assume an attitude of benevolent detachment toward their works, as if they could not care less how others would judge them, and although Merton liked to do this occasionally himself, he nevertheless displayed a normal sensitivity to the quality of the books which he had produced. In a moment I will have something to say about the fact that he was exposed to virtually no real criticism during his life, for which his writing suffered. Be that as it may, in the absence of outer voices he listened to his inner voice, and became his own critic. As such, he probably was much harder on his work than anyone else would have been. The year before he died he drew up an evaluation sheet of thirty of his books, ranging from *Thirty Poems* published in 1944, to *Mystics and Zen Masters* published in 1967; each work was placed in one of seven categories: Best, Better, Good, Fair, Poor, Bad and Awful. He rated none of the thirty books a Best. Thirteen he considered as Better, among which were *The Seven Storey Mountain, Seeds of Contemplation* and *The Sign of Jonas* (with which I agree), and also *Raids on the Unspeakable* and *Conjectures of a Guilty Bystander* (with which I am reluctant to agree). A Good rating was assigned to six books, and five were called Fair. It was surprising that he put *The Ascent to Truth* among the latter, a book which is at least Good. He concluded that three of his books were Poor, including one of his best, *The Living Bread*. Two biographies did not fare well at all. *Exile Ends in Glory* (the life of Mother M. Berchmans, a Trappistine nun) was put in the Bad category, and *What Are These Wounds?* (the life of St. Lutgarde of Aywieres) was pronounced Awful and cast into the exterior darkness.

What this little exercise displays, if nothing else, is that Merton did not look upon his works as in any way sacrosanct. His judgments are for the most part sound, but he had a tendency to underrate some of his early works. He had become toward the end of his life somewhat uncomfortable with the fact that many people regarded him as primarily a "spiritual" or "inspirational" writer—terms which he seemed to regard as pejorative. He appeared definitely embarrassed about many of his early works, and he expressed the opinion that he wished he had not written some of them. He also said that he wanted to be recognized as someone besides the man who wrote *The Seven Storey Mountain*; that man was dead he claimed. The living Merton had moved on to other things. One must take such pronouncements, if not with a grain of salt, at least with a great deal of caution. He liked to exaggerate to make a point, in this case, that he had written several books as good as if not better than *The Seven Storey Mountain*. But he was never able to minimize it to the degree to which its centrality to his entire canon was denied. Indeed, it is important to realize to what extent *The Seven Storey Mountain* is his focal work. Not only does it represent the most moving bit of sustained writing he did, but it contains within it the germs of so many of the ideas he was later to develop and which were to become critical to his world view. In this respect it can be said that the "Thomas Merton" of *The Seven Storey Mountain* did not die at all; he simply grew up.

Even so, one can sympathize with his not wanting constantly to be held responsible at every turn for something which he had written years ago. A writer is not a writer if he is not convinced that he is developing. The best book is always the one which has yet to be written. As to his embarrassment over his early hagiographical and biographical works, in many ways it was warranted. *Exile Ends in Glory* and *What Are These Wounds?* do at times lapse into the kind of syrupy sentimentality which was once in vogue but over which we now rightly blush. For all that, however, even these books are brightened by the uninhibited enthusiasm for the religious life which characterized Merton's early years in the monastery and which contributed so much to making *The Seven Storey Mountain* the fine book it is. He may have been naive in some of these early works, but he was also unquestionably and disarmingly sincere. I have the impression that when he wrote he was conscious of the work immediately before him and virtually oblivious of any audience it subsequently might have. In his later period as a writer Merton became considerably more conscious of his audience, and as a result more conscious of the image he was putting forth. Undeniably this had its favorable repercussions, particularly in that his style was brought under stricter control, at least in those pieces which were not released prematurely. But there were times when the tone was not ringing as true as it had in earlier works. Books like *The Behavior of Titans* and *Raids on the Unspeakable*, for example, display on the whole a pretentiousness, a strained rather than spontaneous informality which one does not find in *The Seven Storey Mountain* and *The Waters of Siloe*. These latter, though technically inferior to the former, have an *élan*, an immediacy, which quickly captivates the reader.

When we attempt to explain Merton's popularity as a writer, it is well not to neglect the element of style. Merton was widely read in great part because of the simple fact that it is a pleasure to read him. For all the particular flaws one could find in his style, it is, taken as a whole, graceful and eminently readable. I have already said that Merton was not a stylist; but he certainly had a style, and a good one at that. Not everyone thought so, of course. Merton tells us that one of his fellow monks, whose job it was to read his manuscripts before they were sent off to the publisher, recommended after finishing *The Seven Storey Mountain* that Merton brush up on his basic English grammar—a fine suggestion to make to a man with two degrees in English from Columbia! Apparently Evelyn Waugh was also a bit taken aback by the loose, rambling style of that book, and as a gesture of good will sent him a copy of Fowler's *Modern English Usage* to peruse. One could easily accept that kind of advice from a master prose stylist like Waugh, and Merton did. But style is the man, as Buffon has sagely reminded us, and Merton could no more write like Waugh, or Henry James, or Cardinal Newman, than he could have become these men.

Merton wrote more after the manner of a Herman Melville or a Thomas Wolfe. A grammarian with a superiority complex could have a heyday going through a Wolfe novel with a blue pencil because they are full of grammatical *faux pas*. But somehow the reader does not seem to notice them once Wolfe's hypnotic process is under way and he is carried off into the author's large sad world on wave after flamboyant wave of magic, majestical words. It is somewhat the same with Merton. Books like *The Seven Storey Mountain, Seeds of Contemplation* and *The Sign of Jonas* pick the reader up and carry him along effortlessly. But unlike Wolfe's, the style of these books is unobtrusive; it does not call attention to itself. It leads immediately into the heart of the author's message.

Therein lies the key to the effectiveness, even brilliance, of Merton's style: it does not call attention to itself. When one reads someone like Henry James, or to a lesser degree, Waugh, one often finds it difficult to grasp the *what* is being said for the *how* it is being said. In other words, style in these authors very much makes its presence felt; it often distracts, and sometimes it even obstructs. The perfect style would be one in which meaning and expression are so masterfully blended that the reader is virtually unconscious of the difference between the two. I will not say that Merton possessed a perfect style, but I will say that he was able to write in such a way that primary importance was always given to the *what* was being said.

Specifically, there were three characteristics which marked his style: it was concrete; it was conversational; and it contained a healthy amount of humor. For most of his life Merton maintained a theoretical antipathy towards abstraction, the obsession for which he regarded as the cause of much of the world's ills. Saturation bombing of civilian populations, for example, can only be carried out, he concluded, when the people in those cities are no longer looked upon as human beings but simply as abstractions—the enemy, the Japs, or 57,123. If given the choice, one should always prefer the concrete over the abstract because by adhering to the concrete one stands in less danger of losing hold of one's humanity; and this is as applicable to style as to anything else. His preference for the concrete was manifested practically in his own style. His vocabulary was precise and down to earth, well calculated to get the idea across to the reader as directly and unambiguously as possible. Even when he was writing about difficult and highly complex subjects, he consistently used the simplest, clearest words he could find.

One never gets the impression in reading Merton of being talked down to. There is nothing stodgy or forbiddingly formal about his writing. It consistently displays the relaxed immediacy of the conversation. To sustain this conversational tone is no mean feat, and yet it is common to most of his books, even those, like *The Ascent to Truth*, which have a fairly formal object in mind. It is this more than anything else which makes his books easy to read, which lends their style its effortless flow. This and the abiding sense of humor which one finds throughout Merton. I will have occasion to talk about this subject at greater length later. For now I will simply say that it was Merton's ability to see first what was funny about himself which made him so quick to detect the humor in the world about him. His sense of humor was not overt—not guffawing and back-slapping, so to speak—but rather Celtic and sly. Through it he draws the reader deftly to himself, for there is no easier and more effective way of winning confidence and breaking down barriers than eliciting a smile or a chuckle. Humor is perhaps the most reliable sign of humanness. But he also used his sense of humor as a means of emphasizing a point, sometimes a very serious point. This is a quite effective literary device, as proven by a novel like Joseph Heller's *Catch-22*. Laughing calls our attention to things we may have been oblivious of, and we begin to notice them, and think about them, in ways we had not done before.

In sum, Merton's prose style was a very accurate reflection of the man behind it—honest, straightforward, unquestionably sincere.

Though a good writer, Merton would have been a better one had the response of his audience been different from what it was. It was too exclusively positive. In the early part of his career he was pretty much a "Catholic writer," which meant not only that his books were stamped with the *imprimatur* and *nihil obstat*, but that his readers were in the main Roman Catholic. In itself, there was nothing wrong with this. If anything, Merton's influence contributed substantially to the maturation of Catholicism in America. By the middle of this century the Catholic Church in this country was coming into its own. Almost a quarter of the total population was in its ranks and it was growing steadily. Though still very self-conscious, it had lost a great deal of its nervous defensiveness; there no longer seemed to be a need to prove at every turn that one could be a good Catholic and a loyal American as well. Catholics were beginning to feel more at home, getting better educated and expanding their interests; to their delight they discovered that there was more to be concerned with than bingo and bricks and mortar. One of the things Catholics became interested in was the status of Catholic intellectualism. After World War II more and more American Catholics began earnestly to ask questions like, Where are our Catholic intellectuals? or, What is a Catholic novelist? Any Catholic writer at the time who showed even the slightest signs of qualifying as an intellectual could be assured of an attentive audience. He was bound to sell books.

This receptive mood which then prevailed is a partial explanation for the success of *The Seven Storey Mountain*. But the audience which welcomed Merton with open arms was not as discriminating as it was enthusiastic, which was to be expected. American Catholic intellectualism was in its infant stages twenty-five years ago, and it is understandable that it was often naively precipitous in what it responded to. Discrimination is a quality of maturity. As a result of this climate, Merton was almost immediately made a Catholic *cause célèbre*. Given Merton's very real talents as well as his sound qualifications as an intellectual, there is of course justification for this; many of his early books were very impressive and worthy of praise. *Seeds of Contemplation*, for example, is a masterpiece of meditative writing, and deserved its large sales. But the point is that virtually none of his early works (by which I mean those published before 1960) were ever really criticized, in the best sense of that term. The mere fact that they were written by a bona fide Catholic intellectual and poet was sufficient for most Catholics.

Most of the articles written during the forties and fifties on Merton's works can scarcely be called critical. They are exercises in adulation for the most part, and in their tone one detects the parochial glee which follows upon the conviction that "one of our boys" has made it big. This almost complete lack of discriminating response to his writing was, I think, a disservice to Merton, for, as is the case with every writer, he could have benefited from some intelligent criticism. Even when criticism is off the mark in its assessments, if it has any pertinence at all it can provide a writer with a helpful sounding board by which he can measure his future work.

What is all the more unfortunate about the unqualified way in which Merton was accepted by the mass of his early audience is that he was quite capable of benefiting from an opposite situation. One of the most apparent manifestations of Merton's humility was his willingness to recognize, and attempt to change, the flaws in his art. I have already mentioned his willingly following Evelyn Waugh's critical advice. Another clear indication of this was his reaction to one of the few pieces of adverse commentary directed against his early work, that written by the Benedictine Dom Aelred Graham. In an article he wrote for the *Atlantic Monthly* (January 1953), Father Graham treated Merton rather roughly, describing him as belonging to that class of writers who are "intense, one-sided, humorless, propagandist, morally indignant." Besides the fact that he was dead wrong in thinking him "humorless," he did hit the mark in calling attention to the sometimes uncompromising brand of Merton's unworldliness. For all that it did not reflect his truest self, there was often in Merton's early writings a rankling holier-than-thou attitude that left the reader with the impression that only those in Trappist monasteries were on the right road to salvation. Significantly, Merton responded positively to this criticism, and to his critic. In later work we clearly detect an absence of the early smugness; he becomes less intransigent on many matters, especially in his attitude toward the world. And he and Father Graham became rather close friends. Such was Merton's ability to respond efficaciously to genuine criticism.

It might even be argued that he was too responsive at times, too eager to defer to opinions about his work which were really not worth paying attention to. This, at least, is what I think was often the case during the sixties. One of Merton's closest friends once said that among his dominant characteristics, which was as apparent during the last year of his life as it was when he was a student at Columbia, was an overriding desire to be "one of the boys." I accept this description with qualifications, but I think it may be helpful in explaining his later reaction to real or imagined criticism. He allowed himself simplistically to take sides with particular audiences, straining too hard to ingratiate himself with people by assuring them that he was totally sympathetic with their cause, standing with them against the "others." This comes out in many of his letters, and the theoretical pattern for this attitude is established in his essay, "Letter to an Innocent Bystander."

But to think Merton was being disingenuous in this would be to be mistaken. He did not want to assure South American guerrillas, say, that he was spiritually at one with them simply because he had a deep need to feel wanted, or because he could thus assuage a hunger for vicarious living, but because he truly did feel at one with them. Just as he truly felt at one with friends who were Latin American aristocrats. Reading Merton, one observes that he sometimes confuses the issues by his personal loyalties, and not a few times he flatly contradicts himself, but these observations apply to the ideological super-struction, as it were. Underneath was the constant of a sincere love held for people of diverse sorts and conflicting ideologies. Merton's "kind of people" was all kinds of people.

His audience changed during the sixties, just as his writing did. One might get into a chicken-or-egg-which-came-first argument over the two, but I am inclined to say that it was his altered writing which preceded and also caused the altered audience. Beginning in the mid-fifties (we see the first hints of it in *No Man is an Island*) Merton was beginning to move away from the exclusively religious subjects which occupied his early writing and starting to talk about the world. He began to write about society and, specifically, the two problems which he thought to be the most critical of our times, the race issue and nuclear war. We will discuss at length what he had to say on these subjects in a later chapter. His frankly stated opinions on them served to alter radically the manner in which he was accepted by many of his readers. The Thomas Merton of the sixties was no longer the unquestioned darling of American Catholics.

To many, of course, he remained a hero, and he quickly became one to many young people, Catholics and non-Catholics alike, especially for the forthright stand he took against the Vietnam war. In a relatively short span of time, in the few years that marked the transition from the decade of the fifties to that of the sixties, much was changed within American Catholicism.

The change in the complexion of American Catholicism contributed to the marked change in the complexion of Merton's audience. It was no longer homogeneous. Although I have no statistics to verify this, I have a feeling that many of those who composed his "new" audience, that is, those (mostly young people) who began their reading with works written in the sixties, were for the most part completely ignorant of what he had written during the previous two decades, especially his meditative works. More, I suspect that they read little of what he wrote in the sixties on subjects outside of war and race. This is the only way I can explain the curiously truncated estimates of Merton which one was hearing at the time of his death. What was described was real enough but not whole enough. Many eulogists had selected a certain portion of his thought and writing which appealed to them and neglected the rest, mainly, again, through simple ignorance in more cases than not.

But if many of the admirers of the new Merton had a very imperfect sense of the full sweep of his thought because of their ignorance of the old Merton, there were others who had known and loved his first books only to be utterly scandalized by some of his last. These were people who believed that it was not the province of a priest and monk to address himself to anything which remotely smacked of politics. No matter if these same people might have been admiring listeners to the radio rampages of Father Coughlin, it was neither fitting nor proper that Father Merton should get mixed up in social issues. Some consolation may be drawn from the fact that few saw fit to criticize his views on the race problem. But the war was an altogether different issue.

Merton's sense of humor no doubt allowed him a smile or two over the blindly negative way in which many readers reacted to his writings on social issues, but, metaphorically if not literally, he must have wept as often as he laughed. There is no doubt, given the sensitive person he was, given his propensity to want to be "one of the boys," that the kind of *ad hominem* attacks he was subjected to towards the end of his life hurt a great deal. But when it came down to a choice between being popular and following his conscience there was no question which way he would go. He had not sought popularity in the first place, and when it came to him through his writing it surprised and embarrassed him. He never got used to it completely, although he tried to adjust to it the best he could. When it began to wane he accepted the fact with equanimity, even, one suspects, with a sense of relief.

CHAPTER III

THE FLEETING MUSE

THERE ARE AT LEAST TWO WAYS in which Thomas Merton can be considered a poet. There is the obvious way, by which we take the term in its literal sense: Merton was a writer of poetry; over the course of his life he published several books of poems. It is this literal sense of his being a poet with which we are going to be primarily concered in this chapter, but before getting into that a few words are in order about the other way in which he was a poet, figuratively. He was a poet in this sense to the degree that he lived out—with great intensity in his youth and in a lesser but still detectable manner in later life—the Romantic ideal of the poet as the visionary loner, the individualistic rebel against the conventions of a society which he has rejected. Insofar as this role was unconscious it reflected a natural propensity toward solitude, a bent for working out his acutely felt sense of destiny pretty much on his own terms. Insofar as it was conscious its emergence can be traced to the days when he was a student of English literature at Columbia; also insofar as it was conscious it was at times simply a facetious pose rather than a serious role. Considering Merton as a Romantic rebel, can, I think, be helpful in coming to a better understanding of various aspects of his life. For example, on a purely natural plane, his decision to enter a Trappist monastery is explained in part by this factor. His role as Romantic rebel also had an important bearing on his literal identity as a poet, in a rather surprising way, however, for it seemed to exert more of an influence upon his later poetry than his earlier.

Though he was ultimately going to argue that poetry is not intended to communicate conceptual formulas, his always did; which is just another way of saying that it was always "about" something. This is a case in point where there is a discrepancy between the artist's theorizing about his art and his practice of it, a happy discrepancy I might say, for when it came to poetry Merton's practical instincts were usually more reliable than his critical theories. He also maintained that poetry should not be didactic, certainly a commonly held view, but not one that could hold up under much serious scrutiny. Better to side with Allen Tate, who once claimed that the only good poetry is didactic poetry.

Despite protestations to the contrary, then, Merton's poetry definitely was "about" something, and often in a distinctly didactic manner. If we survey the entire body of his poetry we can note the recurrence of several themes, four of which are important enough to point out and pause over. There is a sense in which all his poetry is religious poetry, in that it is an expression of his single-minded and overriding concern with ultimate questions. He had ended *The Seven Storey Mountain* with the statement, *sit finis libri, non finis quaerendi* "the book is ended but not the search." The search, Merton's life-long preoccupation, was the search for God, a search carried out through all his writing but especially his poetry. As it was made explicit in subjects having to do with the multiform aspects of the supernatural, we have the specifically religious or transcendental theme in that poetry. Nature was another important theme in Merton's poetry. It would not be correct to think of him as a "nature poet" in the manner of a William Cullen Bryant or other lesser Romantics, for whom nature often became a kind of *ersatz* albeit completely unsatisfactory divinity. For Merton nature, the created universe, was one of the most immediate and stunning signs of the presence of God. The Franciscan in him saw nature as one vast sacrament; for the pure of heart, those with eyes to see and ears to hear, it was a means by which the soul could be brought into contact with the God whose creation it was.

A third important theme in Merton's poetry is anti--modernism. That is the most comprehensive term I could think of to embrace the other "anti's" which his poetry reflects: anti-urbanism, anti-technology and anti-Americanism. All of these are interconnected and often overlap. The most characteristic aspect of the modern age, its identifying soul, was technology, which he abhorred because of its dehumanizing attributes. The city was the focal point for technology, hence to be avoided; the city often stood in his poetry as the central symbol for all which was evil in modern society. Finally, Merton was anti-American in the sense that this country was to him the epitome of modernity with its prevalent urban culture and total dedication to technology and mindless materialism—in a word, everything which he thought was wrong-headed and morally dangerous in the modern world. His anti-Americanism was of the type, as we see in his poem "A Letter to America," which lamented an America gone astray, a country and culture drifted far away from the ideals upon which it was founded. He was saddened by the physical and moral decay he saw across the land because it marked a loss of original innocence; the present situation provided an abundance of sober proof that the dream had thus far gone unfulfilled. Was it too late for a recovery? If not, no comeback was going to happen overnight for "No few fast hours can drain your flesh/Of all those seas of candied poison." A reversal, if it should come, would be more a result of divine intervention than human machinations.

In his prose writings Merton qualified many of the blunt, negative attitudes he had toward the modern world, but poetry is primarily the language of emotion and in his poetry we are informed how he feels about these subjects and not how he thinks about them.

The final major theme I detect in his poetry, and which has close connections with that just discussed, is the apocalyptic theme. This is a theme, of course, which is by no means restricted to his poetry. Merton was an apocalyptic thinker. Which means what? In explaining his rationale for calling this an apocalyptic age he provides us with an answer. "Our times can be called apocalyptic, in the sense that we seem to have come to a point at which all the hidden, mysterious dynamism of the 'history of salvation' revealed in the Bible has flowered into final and decisive crisis." Did he believe that the literal end of the world, in the biblical sense, was near at hand? I do not think we can absolutely preclude the possibility that at least a part of him entertained this thought, but he did take care to point out that the "end of the world" may or may not be a term we can understand—a way of avoiding the issue of literalness. At any rate, this was unquestionably one of his most important metaphors. The evil in the world had reached flood stage; something had to give; some dramatic reckoning was in the offing by which things would be set straight. His second book of poems, *Figures for an Apocalypse* is one in which, as the title makes obvious, the apocalyptic theme is predominant. In the central poem of the book New York, the modern city, is destroyed in a roaring holocaust. Merton had a way of artistically taking care of those things for which he had little admiration. Though his apocalyptic vision was obviously in great part theologically informed, it was not exclusively so. Contemporary literature abounds with apocalyptic writers, most of whom have no discernible religious convictions and many of whom have probably never even read St. John. In a world where there are enough nuclear warheads to blow us all to smithereens several times over you do not have to be especially religious to be convinced that the end of the world is near.

In considering other poets who influenced Merton's poetry, one has to proceed with the care which should accompany any discussion of literary influences. It is a subject one should hesitate to be dogmatic about. Given the fact that he wrote his master's thesis on him, and consequently read him extensively and studied him carefully, it is safe to say that Merton was influenced by William Blake; but, I hasten to add, more in terms of themes, of sharing Blake's *Weltanschauung*, than in terms of style. Merton's early poetry especially reflects Blake's adamant otherworldly view, his general mystical orientation. Indeed, Merton's anti-modernism is something which can be traced to Blake. Style was an altogether different matter, however; Merton was never capable of the crisp, controlled expression characteristic of Blake's poetry. Brevity was simply not his forte, in poetry or in prose. T.S. Eliot was another conscious influence upon Merton's poetry. As a matter of fact, at one point in his career, discouraged over the quality of his poetry, he decided that he was either going to have to learn to write like Eliot or give it up entirely. He did neither. He was influenced by Eliot thematically (his anti-modernism owed as much to him as it did to Blake) as well as stylistically; as far as the latter kind of influence was concerned it was for the most part unfortunate. Merton brought his poetic language under better control *à la* Eliot, but without being able to match Eliot's inner vision. The result was a forced, stiff and ultimately unconvincing product. "The Tower of Babel" strikes me as a particularly unhappy result of Merton's attempt to write like Eliot. In the end, Eliot's influence was more detrimental to Merton than beneficial, for it diverted him from his main task as a poet—the discovery and development of his own voice.

One cannot read a line like, "Father, the world bursts, breaks, huge Spirit, with Thy might" (and there are many more like it), with its insistent alliteration and scarcely containable joy, without realizing that he was substantially influenced by Gerard Manley Hopkins as well. And when I see the way he liked to develop complex and clever analogues between physical facts and spiritual realities (the poem "Nature" provides a good example), I detect possible influential links with the "metaphysical" poets of the 17th century, especially with John Donne, and George Herbert. Finally, though here I speak with considerably less confidence, I see in some of his last poetry hints of the style of Gertrude Stein.

Taking the story of Thomas Merton's poetry as a whole, that is, from the publication of his first book in 1944 to the publication of his last, posthumously, in 1969, the most striking feature about it is the periodically fluctuating, but over the long run steady deterioration in artistic quality. Unlike

Robert Frost's, Merton's poetry did not strengthen and mature with the years. A brief recounting of the story of his poetry allows me to discuss in more detail Merton's poetic gift as well as to trace the pattern of this gradual falling off of artistic quality. The pattern once traced, I would like, finally, to offer some explanations for it.

His first book, *Thirty Poems*, came out, as already noted, in 1944. It was followed hard behind by *A Man in the Divided Sea* (1946) and *Figures for an Apocalypse* (1947). There is, to be sure, a good deal of imperfection in all of these works, but that is offset and sometimes obliterated by the freshness, spontaneity and utter earnestness of the poet's voice. In these early poems Merton showed where his real skill lay, as a lyricist. He proved himself to be a singer. He may not have always been on tune, maybe his voice was occasionally a bit gravelly, but he sang with a captivating conviction and enthusiasm. The early Merton was an effusive poet; he often overwrote. But sometimes his effusiveness was his best asset, and he could, if not bowl you over, at least bend you decisively, by sheer verbal verve. Listen to a few lines from a poem called "April":

Hear how like lights these following releases
Of sharpened shaft-lights sing across the air,
And play right through, unwounding, clearest windworks
To disappear, unpublished, in the reeds.

One might be able to pick away at defects in technique in a passage like this without being able to take a thing away from the freedom, the lilting vitality—in a word, the irrepressible poetry—which is its essential characteristic. When Merton was working well with his muse, he could have a masterful way with words. They fell into lines which seemed well-nigh perfect for their balance, wit and sonic surprises. "Figures for an Apocalypse" provides such a line: "What flame flares in the jaws of the avenging mills! "

It is not necessary to read a great deal of Merton's poetry to recognize that the simile was by far and away his favorite literary device, and that, furthermore, he preferred to announce the simile by a double "as" rather than by "like."

(Phrases based on the paradigm "as   as   " abound in his poetry.) In all, Merton's use of the simile makes for a very interesting subject, worthy of a separate study. Without going into any great detail, suffice it to say that his similes are very often surprising and pleasing for their imaginativeness and ingenuity. Merton had a penchant for making the comparisons as bizarre and seemingly incongruous as possible, and not unseldom it is this very incongruity which gives them their greatest force, lending them dramatic poignance, such as, for example, in "with eyes as sharp as stones." Sometimes this concerted incongruity backfires, however, and ends up as simple incompatibility. "Eyes as bright as milk, eyes like towers, eyes as mad as rocks," and "clubs as loud as bells" are all similes which put too great a strain on the imagination. They just do not work.

The Tears of the Blind Lions (1949) was Merton's fourth book of poetry. It was a slim little volume, containing only seventeen poems, most of which are quite solid. "To the Immaculate Virgin, on a Winter Night" is particularly noteworthy. Yet this book lacks the suppleness, the almost sassy bravado of the first three. Merton's tone begins to assume a tinge of painful self-consciousness. We note here a general stiffening up. His voice seems a bit forced at times, at times a bit hollow. One has the impression that at this juncture Merton might have been paying undue attention to models and not sufficiently cultivating his own poetic garden. Also to be considered is the fact that around the time this book was being written—1948-49—he was beginning to lose faith in himself as a poet. Perhaps he had been deceived all along, thinking that he had genuine talent. "I certainly find it extremely difficult," he said in *The Sign of Jonas*, "to believe in myself as a poet." He found it so difficult, and also began to worry about the people whom he might be leading astray, that he decided (and not for the first time) he was going to quit writing poetry altogether. The greatest danger he saw, should he continue, would be that ultimately he might convince himself that he was truly a poet when in fact he was not. So, he obtained permission from his abbot and stopped writing poetry, for a while. It was not too long before he was at it once again however. Thus we witness a rather common occurrence in Merton's literary life: the dramatic and emphatic putting behind of this, that or the other, only eventually to return to it once again. This seemed to be one of the ways he kept himself alert to what he was doing. It was an antidote against perfunctoriness.

His first four books of poetry were published within five years. Eight years were to pass between the publication of the fourth and fifth. *The Strange Islands* (1957) continued to display the stiffening, overly-formalistic tendencies which had begun to show up in *The Tears of the Blind Lions.* I think one of the chief reasons for this is that he was giving too great an ear to others and not developing his own proper voice. We note a decided lack of spontaneity. The poems in this volume are by and large under much better control than those he had written previously, and this, needless to say, was not altogether bad. But too often they lack fire. A lot of the careless verbal effusiveness was now gone, but with it the emotional intensity which inspired it. Too, for the first time in his poetry, we see him introducing esoteric elements whose function is not always clear; much of it, indeed, seems simply gratuitous. It is as if Merton were toying with the idea of becoming a "difficult poet" but could not completely make up his mind on the subject.

Though my judgment on this matter may be off, I have long considered "The Tower of Babel," a long verse play described as a morality, to be the low point of the book; it is completely unconvincing, and the reason this is so is because it is not really Merton. It is an uninspired, almost slavish imitation of Eliot, both in theme and style. This is all too bad, because the ideas behind the play are good and something significant might have been made of them. There is substance to be reckoned with, for example, in lines like: "Words have always been our best soldiers./They have defeated meaning in every engagement/And have almost made an end of reality."

But for all its weaknesses, *The Strange Islands* is not a disaster. It has in it some competent poems, such as "The Guns of Fort Knox." (The poem has a special significance for me now because I wrote this particular chapter at the Abbey of Gethsemani, and as I wrote I could hear—as Thomas once heard and was inspired by—the ominous sound of the guns of Fort Knox, booming across the Kentucky hills.) And several poems which in their entirety are not too impressive nevertheless contain poignant and memorable passages. A great deal of instinctive insight stands behind two lines from "How to Enter a Big City." The poet observes that, "Everywhere there is optimism without love/And pessimism without understanding." The observation could apply to many places and many times, but it seems particularly applicable to the America of the 1950s from which it emerged.

In 1959 a volume of selected poems was published. It was a good selection; he picked his better poems for it. Given my own judgment of his poetry, it is noteworthy that of the seventy-one selections which this book contains, fifty-two come from his first three books, *Thirty Poems, A Man in the Divided Sea* and *Figures for an Apocalypse. Original Child Bomb,* which came out two years later, in 1961, does not easily classify according to a specific literary genre. It was billed by the publisher as a poem, but not a few critics, and with cause, refused to accept the designation. There is no need to get into a froth over the matter, however, for a happy and accurate compromise can be made by calling it a prose-poem. Its language is prose; its tone is poetic. Put another way, it expresses in ordinary language the extraordinary dimensions of an essentially poetic message. To say the work is impressive and forceful is to put it mildly. It may well be the most trenchant piece of satire in modern American literature. With disarming simplicity and unadorned directness the work recounts the circumstances that led up to the dropping of the first atomic bomb by the United States. The end result is an emphatic condemnation of this act, a condemnation made all the more devastating by the subtle, masterfully understated tone that Merton maintains throughout. These "points for meditation to be scratched on the walls of a cave" deserve to be known more widely than they are.

Merton's sixth poetic work, *Emblems of a Season of Fury*, published in 1963 (there is a somber appropriateness to the title, given the fact that this was the year John Kennedy was assassinated), shows a promising upturn in what was otherwise a descending pattern of poetic development. He seems to have been coming to terms with his new voice, which is to say that the austerer, more controlled language was beginning to show something besides austerity and control. It was showing signs of life, becoming less tense and unconvincing. It was as if, now, the control was emerging from within the language rather than being arbitrarily forced upon it from without. In a word, the language was more natural. The book contains several fine poems, such as the touching and tonally perfect "An Elegy for Ernest Hemingway." Another poem, "Chant to be Used in Processions around a Site with Furnaces," gives further evidence of Merton's powers as a satirist From it we can get an indication of what he might have done along this line, had he not decided, in his two subsequent books, to follow an altogether different course. *Emblems of a Season of Fury* is unusual in that about half of it is devoted to his translations of other poets. He translated Raissa Maritain from the French and several South American poets from the Spanish. His abilities as a translator of Spanish verse have been highly touted, and at least one knowledgeable critic considered him among the best in the world.

If *Emblems of a Season of Fury* showed some promise, some signs, shall we say, of definite poetic progress, the situation was reversed with *Cables to the Ace* (1968). In order to understand this book and the posthumously published *The Geography of Lograire*, which appeared a year later, it is essential to understand that something very important happened to Merton's conception of himself as poet before these books were written. He became an anti-poet. An anti-poet, as he defined the term, was a person who wrote anti-poetry—that is, a barely intelligible mimic of conventional poetry—as a form of protest against what was considered to be the "sell-out" to the Establishment on the part of conventional poets. Anti-poetry was a deliberate and conscious abuse of language. Meaning was sent scurrying to the battlements and promptly put under siege. An early passage in the book notes, "Some of the better informed have declared war on language." How could one describe the end results of this experiment? In all, pretty bad. What we see in the *Cables to the Ace* is that loss of wholeness without which no literary work can make pretentions toward poetry. Erratic, disjointed, this is a case study of fragmentation; things fall apart for the same reason which Yeats once pointed out: the center does not hold. There are sporadic moments of brightness in the book—some of the language is witty and incisive—but because we are dealing with a hodgepodge, there is no consistent, coherent context in which these moments can properly illuminate one another. They shine in isolation. This is all the more unfortunate because one of the important thematic elements of the book thus vitiated is the allusion to several critical contemporary political issues. Merton's intent, again, is to satirize, but the satire fails because the message is garbled. For all that, however, the book is significant for its implicit social criticism, as well as for the presence in it of distinctive Oriental, specifically Zen, influences. This latter theme, as I shall point out in greater detail in a later chapter, reflected a major preoccupation within Merton's thought at this time. The language of the book does, as I said, display some creativity and cleverness, but this is the exception rather than the rule. By and large it drags. Merton attempts to establish a brusk, swaggering nonchalance, which in fact comes across as a kind of decrepit 1940's jive talk whose misfortune it often is gradually to ossify and stumble into pure and—for the reader—painful corniness. "These words were once heard, uttered by a lonely, disembodied voice, seemingly in a cloud. No one was impressed by them and they were immediately forgotten."

    The Geography of Lograire takes up where *Cables to the Ace* left off—in a semantic no man's land. The first thing which has to be said about this book, publishing notices to the contrary, is that it is not a poem. While something unfinished can be poetic, nothing unfinished can be called a poem.

A poem is a work of art whose identity waits upon the sense of aesthetic completeness announced by the "click" which, at least according to Yeats, the poet hears when the work is finally and unquestionably finished. This work is presented to us as avowedly unfinished. What we discover in it is the work of a clever arranger, but not a poet. A lot of the material for the book is borrowed in large quantities from other sources; quotations are abundant and paraphrases are common. Now we all know that some of the greatest of poets frankly and unapologetically borrowed material from sources other than their own imaginations, and I am not faulting Merton for the simple fact of his being a borrower. However, what we have here is something distinctively different from the kind of literary pilfering which every artist indulges in. Most poets take ideas from hither and yon, then attempt to recast them in their own stylistic images, to assimilate them and make them a part of their own aesthetic self. Merton does this occasionally here, it is true, but what he does more often is to bring in piecemeal hefty portions of other people's work. The artistic purpose which is served by this is far from clear and I am inclined to think that it is a sign that Merton was definitely tiring as a poet, that the old doubts about his abilities were existentially working themselves out in his literary productions. Like *Cables to the Ace*, this book is fragmented and disjointed; its points of view are fuzzy and consequently confusing. And the fact that these things were consciously intended does not lessen their adverse effect. The book is laden with allusions which are as a rule remote and esoteric; to keep up with them the reader has to cease to be a reader and become a sleuth. I can imagine the work one day becoming the favorite artifact of the more morbid professors in graduate schools of English, especially those who teach courses like Introduction to Graduate Study. It presents many "problems," gratuitously more often than not, without solving the biggest one—that of its own aesthetic *raison-d'être*.

I think it was St. Thomas Aquinas who once observed that no book is all bad. The observation is as true of *The Geogra-*

phy of Lograire as of any other. "East," the first section of the work, moves along well due to sprightly, properly tempered language, and it is interesting. "Day Six O'Hare Telephone" is worth extracting and acknowledging as an individual poem of considerable merit. In a way, it is really old hat Merton, for it dutifully reflects the varying aspects of the anti-modernism which was part and parcel of his poetry from the beginning. When he gets onto this familiar subject the focus begins to clear; images are vivid and nicely interlock to form a coherent, convincing whole. The poem has bite, verve.

No matter what one might finally think of it, the very nature of this book—wide-ranging, rambling, obstinately but obscurely suggestive—is such that discussion of it can go on interminably, and probably get no further than it might have gotten in the first five minutes. (There seems to be a correlation between the confusion of the poem and the confusion of criticisms written about it, in this respect; critics who proclaim the volume as a great work of art appear to be uniformly incapable of giving reasons for the proclamation.) But the most important question which ultimately has to be asked of the book is this: Should a book which has been described by the author as "a purely tentative first draft of a longer work in progress" be published at all? Given my own strongly held views on the essentialness of aesthetic completeness to a poem, I would unhesitantly say no. The admitted tentativeness of the book is, indeed, the explanation for most of its problems; at any rate, I feel it explains most of the faults I find with it. In the final analysis, there is not much you can do with a "purely tentative first draft" besides passing a purely tentative judgment on it—a purely tentative judgment which is doomed to remain, by the very nature of the case, a *permanently* purely tentative judgment. This is the kind of paradoxical critical denouement which Merton would have appreciated.

So much for the story of his poetry, briefly told, as it developed over a span of twenty-five years. That development, I reiterate, was not altogether a happy one. It started off fairly well but then began to falter as Merton, seeking to trim his stylistic sails and assume a more modest voice, lost much of the charming, albeit at times naive, *élan* which characterized his earliest work. It looked as though he had recovered himself in *Emblems of a Season of Fury*, that he had found his proper, mature voice, but the book had raised false hopes. *Original Child Bomb* was distinguished but his last two books were not. And if these last two books were disappointments it was primarily because of Merton's decision to take on the role of anti-poet. That decision, artistically speaking, was a bad one.

It was a bad decision because it was based on a fundamental misapprehension of events. We recall that the guiding rationale behind the writing of anti-poetry is that it serves as a form of protest against the conventional verse of poets who have become subservient to the political and cultural powers that be. In such a situation conventional poetry became tainted—representing a kind of literary guilt by complicity— and the man of integrity could not practice it. Merton more than once expressed the opinion that what he called the "academic" poets in America were the dupes of the Establishment, and it was presumably against these, or for the benefit of these, he was writing his anti-poetry. But who these establishmentarian academic poets were, I would give worlds to know. Merton never named names, and I suspect for good reason: he could not have, or at least not many, and they would not be very important names after all. The fact of the matter is that during the decade of the sixties it was the academic poets (e.g., Louis Simpson, John Berryman, Galway Kinnell, James Wright, W. D. Snodgrass, Donald Hall) and the para-academic poets (Robert Bly, Denise Levertov, Robert Lowell) who were the most vociferous and adamant anti-establishmentarians, especially in the matter of the Vietnam war. It is difficult to see, then, what Merton was jousting against in his anti-poetic forays, apart from figments of his own imagination. I suspect that what he most probably did was extrapolate from situations in other countries and conclude, without really knowing the facts, that those conditions applied equally as well here.

It was a bad decision, secondly, because it was logically unsound. The premise upon which anti-poetry is based—that you counteract poetry which has become divorced from meaning by writing other meaningless poetry— simply will not stand up under close examination. You do not restore integrity to language by rendering it virtually incomprehensible. To attempt to defeat meaninglessness by more meaninglessness is to use the kind of self-defeating weapon St. Augustine talks about: that which must pass through your heart first. Both "poet" and anti-poet end up slain, and for what purpose, other than the possible satisfaction of a petty vindictiveness?

To succumb to the kind of non-solution represented by anti-poetry was to succumb to a kind of double-think which, in other circumstances, Merton was eminently alert to and courageously against. The most perplexing thing about his assuming the stance of anti-poet is that, in fact, it went against some of his own, often stated, best instincts. He specifically warned other poets, especially those who looked up to him, to guard against using language as a weapon to bludgeon the enemy rather than a tool to communicate. "The artist who expends all his efforts in convincing himself that he is not a non-artist or the anti-artist who struggles not to become 'an artist,' cannot justify his vexations by appealing to an ideal of freedom."

Given Merton's attitude toward the subject, anti-poetry comes across, almost by definition, more as a tactic than an art form. It is a means of besting— or at least discrediting— the other guy by methods which, if circumstances were different, would presumably not be used. You are, in other words, using the tactics of the enemy to beat him at his own game. But, again, as Merton showed himself to be fully aware in other matters, this has its disadvantages as well as its clear dangers. One recalls his attitude just previous to the full outbreak of World War Two. He feared America's entry into the war because, as he reckoned, in order to defeat the Nazis she would have to become like them. This is the price one pays for fighting a totally unscrupulous foe. I do not intend onerously to overdramatize the analogy between this circumstance and Merton's writing anti-poetry, but one can at least wonder if a precious amount of artistic self is not surrendered by turning your art into a vehicle for exorcising the demons of unmeaning by what appears to be a planned program of verbal magic.

Aside from the theoretical weaknesses of such a program, there remain the very large practical problems of, one, distinguishing between the sold-out and unsold-out poets so you know whom to oppose (a distinction, as we have seen, Merton did not clearly make) and, two, determining what constitutes conventional verse. In a day when there is a great deal of experimentation in verse this latter could pose some substantial difficulties. Finally—and this is not at all an absurd possibility, given the rapidity with which what is radical is blessed by the mass media and swept into the main stream—what happens when anti-poetry becomes conventional? Do you then go back to traditional forms because that is now clean? One can envision the poet, as a result of relying upon a pose rather than concentrating on the development of his own voice, dissipating all his energies in a frantic effort to keep on the opposit side of the fence from those whom he considers artistically compromised.

It is not difficult for me to imagine someone disagreeing with this assessment of Merton's poetry. One could say, for example, that in my critique of *Cables to the Ace* and *The Geography of Lograire* I simply miss the point, that if these two works are fragmented and disjointed it is because they were deliberately intended to be such in order to mirror and pass judgment upon the fragmented and disjointed nature of our age. The message, in other words, is as much in the form as in the content. To stand in judgment of a chaotic age, as a poet and prophet, one must speak chaotically. All I can say in response to this is that I am perfectly aware of the point; it is just that I do not agree with it. One does not intimidate or dispel linguistic chaos by yet more linguistic chaos. I stand with E. B. Strunk who claimed that the only way to cope adequately with confusion was unconfusedly. To write about confusion confusedly only compounds the confusion, and that was what Merton was doing by his anti-poetry.

Do I think Merton was being insincere in writing anti-poetry? Not for a moment. I do not think Thomas Merton had an insincere bone in his body. The decision to become an anti-poet was an expression of his deep concern and worry over the evils which he saw in his world and his total commitment to their destruction. This was his way, specifically as a poet, of putting his life on the line, of announcing to the world that he would not be a party to its evil. But, not withstanding the sincerity which went behind it, the choice was an unfortunate one. It served well neither himself nor poetry. For all that, however, and for his own serious and I think abiding doubts as to his poetic ability, Merton was indeed a poet and a good one. Though his development was arrested, he reached a plane of competence from which he produced works whose value ranks him among the best minor American poets of this century.

CHAPTER IV

THE MONK

ANY ATTEMPT TO UNDERSTAND Thomas Merton which either glosses over or neglects the strategic importance of monasticism in his life is foredoomed to failure. Merton was pre-eminently the monk, and to forget that is to forget altogether too much. If we look at his writings we see that other subjects come and go, or fluctuate in the importance he attached to them over the years, but monasticism remains consistently central to his concerns. From *The Waters of Siloe* (1949) through *The Sign of Jonas* (1953) and *The Silent Life* (1957) to *The Climate of Monastic Prayer* (1969) and *Contemplation in a World of Action* (1971)—just to name major titles—the pattern is clear.

There are many things we can make of Merton's being a monk, that is to say, we can attach various psychological or sociological meanings to his decision to lead a life which, by just about every standard with which we feel comfortable today, has got to be considered rather unusual. I intend to dwell for a moment upon such matters, but before doing so, and for the sake of balance, I think it necessary to admit that the deepest meanings of his vocation as a monk are not going to be found, finally, in that kind of analysis, no matter how carefully done and well-intentioned. There is a large amount of mystery behind a man's decision to live as a monk, and it seems to me that unless we are willing to begin by acknowledging this we can not lay claim to very much objectivity at all. In this sense we must be willing to accept Merton on his own terms, and concede with him that the meaning of his being a monk is explained ultimately by a response to a supernatural grace, a divine call to lead such a life. In a word, Merton chose to be a monk because he felt he had *been chosen* to be a monk. He believed this to be the core factor of his monastic identity, the foundation upon which rested whatever else might be brought to bear on the subject.

This, he realized, was at once an explanation and a nonexplanation, for when you claim you are something because God chose you to be that something then you immediately enter into a realm of mystery where you no longer feel confident in explaining matters, not even to yourself. However, being in the realm of mystery is not the same thing as being in a state of confusion, and a man can willingly admit that his life is shrouded in mystery without being in the least doubtful that that life is the one he should be leading.

Having started with the premise that Merton's monastic life is to be viewed simply as the result of a free decision on his part to follow such a life, based upon a firm conviction of a divine call, there is nothing which says we have to stop there. More about the matter can be said, in particular that his being a monk was in part an expression of Merton the Romantic poet.

Recall it having been noted in the previous chapter that a way of considering Merton a poet, figuratively speaking, was as one who lived out in his life many of the attitudes which were common to the poet of the nineteenth century Romantic tradition. That is to say, he tended to be a loner; he felt alienated by his times, was highly critical of his society; and he put a premium on following that personal daemon which would lead him to his enchanted yet hidden destiny. These are factors which contributed, I believe, though most probably not consciously, to Merton's decision to become a monk, particularly a Trappist monk. The intensely medieval character of the monastery which he entered in December 1941 appealed greatly to his Romantic temperament. The milieu would provide him ample opportunity—or at least so he hoped—to be alone, and in the silence of his soul bring to term all the things which he was destined to be. The very idea of entering a monastery flew in the face of everything which was modern, which is to say, at least as far as Merton was concerned, reprehensible. Monasticism was a living indictment of a world which he, by the time he was twenty-five, had become thoroughly disenchanted with. To live as a monk was to live constantly in protest against that world. It was a most dramatic way of announcing one's repudiation of it. There was, as I say, a good deal of the unconscious Romantic poet in this, but we must also realize that Merton always considered the element of protest to be integral to the monastic life, not the sulking, wounded-pride type of protest common to the Romantic, but rather the robust, clear-headed protest of the prophet. The Romantic repudiates the world because it does not measure up to his expectations; the prophet does so because it does not live according to the law of God. Merton, as monk, was both Romantic and prophet, but never in equal proportions, and his Romantic notions of monasticism are relegated in great part to his early days as a monk. The longer he stayed in the monastery the more mature became his attitude toward monasticism.

Finally, in connection with the Romantic aspects of his vocation, Merton's becoming a monk was a way, as he himself suggested in *The Sign of Jonas,* of insuring himself that life was not going to pass him by, that he was going to confront it head-on and consequently come to a satisfactory conception of what it was all about. This seems ironical, that a man should go to a monastery to confront life, but Merton was not being any more ironical than was Henry David Thoreau who told us—and Merton quotes this statement with obvious admiration and approval: "I went to the woods because I wished to live deliberately, to front only the essential facts of life, and see if I could not learn what it had to teach me and not, when I came to die, discover that I had not lived." Merton had underlined all but the first eight words of the quotation. Thoreau went to the woods of Walden to live deliberately, Merton, to the woods of Kentucky.

The whole idea of becoming a monk is to simplify your

life, to rid it of all the distracting paraphenalia which comes courtesy of the twentieth century, and reduce it to its simplest terms. This accomplished, a man devotes the major portion of his time grappling with life's largest questions—God, love, death, eternal life—the questions which we all dutifully assure ourselves that we are one day going to get around to, when we have time. The monk *makes* time. He makes a deliberate effort to insure that his life is "uneventful," that is, lacking in inane busyness, *divertissement*, so that he will ever be open to life itself. Merton was particularly sensitive about the issue of the simplicity of monastic life. For him the chief reason for pursuing the religious life was to find God, and anything which would hinder that discovery would of necessity have to be considered antipathetic to the religious life. It was a matter of total commitment. In the uncompromising fervor of the Trappist way of life Merton found the kind of total commitment he was looking for. He concluded that the Trappist really meant business, as he did, and in retrospect he saw it as providential that he did not become a Franciscan. The Franciscans were good and earnest people, no doubt, but Merton conjectured that life among then might be altogether too comfortable, too bourgeois. Where would be the sacrifice in such a life?

But Merton was not a Trappist long before he began to show signs that he was less than fully satisfied with the Order. It was not that he found the life too hard; he seemed to have accommodated himself gamely, if not always easily, to the rigorous routine. Rather, he wondered if the thoroughly cenobitic life of the Cistercians, a life in which practically everything during the course of a day was done in common, was the life to which he was best suited. His natural penchant for solitude inspired yearnings for a monastic tradition which allowed more privacy to the individual monk, and eremitic orders such as the Carthusians and Camaldolese began to appeal greatly to him. Apparently it was touch and go for some time whether Merton would in fact leave Gethsemani and join an order of hermits. In the end, however, his superiors prevailed upon him to stay, convincing him that he was where he was supposed to be. He accepted their word in a spirit of obedience, but clearly it was not simply a matter of his gritting his teeth and remaining in a monastery and an order for which he had little real attachment. There is no doubt that he loved the Cistercians, and his love for Gethsemani—although he was later to step up his complaints of the place because he felt it was being turned into something uncomfortably like a factory—was no less. He was, after all, a Cistercian and a monk of Gethsemani. At times, it is true, he had harshly critical things to say about both, but it is also true that we are often most critical of what we most love.

At any rate, though he made up his mind to remain a Cistercian, he did not abandon his attraction for the eremitical life. It did not take him long to discover, committed scholar of monastic history that he was, that the eremitical tradition was not completely foreign to the Cistercian way of life. Though it had not happened since at least the eighteenth century, there had been incidents in which Cistercian monks were given permission to live as hermits. Encouraged by this knowledge, he began in the 1950s a campaign to reestablish this tradition within the Order. His task proved not to be an easy one, for at the time there were not many who were receptive to the idea, and the fact that he persevered in his efforts provides clear evidence of the strength of his commitment to the eremitical ideal. This was obviously no passing fad for him. His labors were rewarded in the 1960s. Early in that decade the abbot allowed for Merton's spending certain periods in a cement block hermitage built in a beautiful wooded area about one mile south of the monastery. Then, in 1965, he was permitted to live there permanently, with one condition: that he take the main meal of the day in the monastery refectory with his fellow monks. The abbot did not want even a hermit completely to sever bonds with the larger community. Merton succeeded in interesting many of his fellow monks in the eremitical life, and it seems to be growing. Interestingly enough, Dom James Fox, who opened the way for Merton to become a hermit, has himself been living as a hermit since his retirement from the abbacy in

1967. And his successor as abbot of Gethsemani, a former student of Merton's and apparently influenced by him in this respect, lived one day of each week in a hermitage.

It is no exaggeration to say that Merton almost single-handedly revived the eremitical tradition within the Cistercian Order. The world at large is aware of Merton and future histories will have occasion to take note of him for a variety of different reasons; but there is a good likelihood that Cistercian historians centuries hence will recognize him primarily as that ebullient American monk who, in the middle of the twentieth century, reintroduced the hermit's life to the Order.

Be that as it may, it scarcely needs arguing that Merton was one of the most enthusiastic and eloquent spokesmen for monasticism in recent times. He sang its praises to his fellow monks, of course, but as his books amply demonstrate, he saw fit to do so for a general audience as well. The reason for this was quite simple: Merton firmly believed that monasticism was an institution which, by its very nature, was highly implicated in the society at large. This at first might seem a rather odd point of view, for by definition monks are people who live apart from their society and, very often, in ideological opposition to it. For Merton, monasticism's implication in and separation from society were both true, and although this might make for a paradoxical situation, it was not necessarily a contradictory one, as I shall attempt to point out.

His attitude toward monasticism, as was true of his attitude toward many things, developed and matured over the years. It is true that when he first came to the monastery he took a rather simplistic view of the institution and the monastic vocation. The world outside the walls was then seen as an almost hopelessly desolate place. In fact one easily gets the impression that Merton felt that it would only be a matter of time before that world, because of its sins, would be destroyed in an apocalyptic rain of fire and brimstone. We recall the poetic suggestion he made to two of his friends in "Figures for an Apocalypse," to get out of New York while there was still time. In contrast to the chaos and evil which was modern society, the monastery was a haven of serenity and holiness where a man could, having washed out of his psyche all the sordid remnants of the world he had left, confidently seek out his salvation. As the years passed this clearly delineated picture, containing a sharp dichotomy between the world and the monastery, grew more complex. As we shall see more fully in the following chapter, Merton began to look upon the world with less jaundiced eyes. He became more open to it. This is not to say that he suddenly recognized it to be a totally marvelous place, and that he had been grossly mistaken all along by thinking that it was evil. No, Merton's view of the world, that is, of contemporary society, never changed substantially, he consistently regarded it as being in a rather sad state of affairs. What did change was his attitude toward what he should be doing about it. As a young monk he settled pretty much upon a laissez-faire policy. Leave the world to its own devilish devices. Let the dead bury their dead. For himself, he had washed his hands of it and was no longer concerned with what was going on "out there." This attitude was eventually replaced by one which accepted a certain amount of responsibility for the evil which was in the world. It was no longer enough for the monk to repudiate that evil; he, precisely as a monk, had to do something to try to overcome it.

At the same time that he was beginning to see his relationship with the world with new eyes, his initial impressions of monasticism began to alter. If in his enthusiam as a novice he saw nothing but the good, eventually he came to realize that the monastic life, like every other life, has its faults. He became especially concerned with the fact that Gethsemani was becoming much too big and boisterous a place, with the consequence that the silence and even pace which he always thought were essential to the monastic way of life were becoming harder and harder to maintain. That Gethsemani was indeed expanding at a dizzying rate was true enough, but this was hardly the result of a deliberate choice on the part of the monks. It must rather be attributed to the phenomenal vocation boom which followed the Second World War, when because of the large number of young men who passed through Gethsemani's gates to become monks, this monastery, originally built for some seventy monks, was in a relatively short span of time housing two-hundred and seventy. No wonder it was noisy! As I said, this expansion was quite unplanned, but without being entirely facetious it might be suggested that Merton himself was in part responsible for it. It seems safe to say that many of those who sought entry in Trappist monasteries, especially Gethsemani, during the early fifties did so because they had read books like *The Seven Storey Mountain* and *The Waters of Siloe.*

But it wasn't just a matter of the monastery becoming oversized. More serious, in Merton's eyes, was a tendency he detected to assume some of the worst aspects of the world. Specifically, he was disturbed by the way monastic life, especially the agricultural part of it, was being thoroughly mechanized. Besides all the disturbing clamor the new machines were creating, they were limiting the monks' immediate contact with the soil and with nature, a contact which he thought essential for a viable life of prayer. Too, he did not like the way the monastery was becoming a "business," producing cheese and fruit cakes for sale on the open market. Once these kinds of enterprises find themselves in operation within the monastery, it is not too long before the monks begin to think and act like businessman—than which, for Merton, nothing could be worse. One of his most persistent prejudices was that against business and businessmen. He regularly used the two terms as pejoratives.

In general, what he saw as the most dangerous trend in modern monasticism, Cistercian monasticism not excluded, was an unconscious opting for bourgeois comfortableness. Toward the end of his life he had a habit of referring to the monk's life, ideally considered, as the vocation of Job. As we know, things did not go too well for Job, but in spite of that he lived firmly in his faith. Merton could not reconcile himself to an interpretation of monastic life as one in which you have practically everything which you could have had in any other life. In such a situation the vow of poverty becomes a scandal, an empty gesture. If a monk lives in a rich monastery, not wanting anything essential and getting plenty which was not essential, steeped in security, how was he really poor? When Merton spoke of monastic reform, as he often did in his later years, this is the problem he often had primarily in mind.

The question inevitably arises, given that Merton criticized, and often trenchantly, his way of life, if he ever considered leaving it. We do not have to exercise much guesswork on this question because Merton himself tells us that he did consider it, but in much the same way that any of us, in a moment of frustration and exasperation, would think of walking out on something that we are doing, or being—only to repent of our precipitousness a moment later, realizing in our heart of hearts that we could no more walk out than fly out. Such was the case with Merton. He said he entertained for five minutes once the thought of leaving the monastery, only to reject the thought as unacceptable. This came in the somber days of the early 1960s, when his superiors were subjecting some of his writings to censorship, a matter we will discuss in the next chapter. Upon reflection, he decided that nothing whatever would be gained by his leaving the monastery, and if he did so it would probably be only to assuage his own pride and not for the sake of truth.

However much Merton might have concerned himself with various practical aspects of monasticism, he knew that its real source of vitality and strength was internal, residing—or lacking—in each individual monk. What was a monk according to his point of view? First of all, a monk emphatically was not simply a man who wore a peculiar garb and followed a set of observances. This was part of it, of course, but not all of it, for someone can put on a robe, and following observances can easily become a perfunctory and spiritless proposition. The most important part of a monk's identity is his subscribing unconditionally to the prospect of *metanoia*, or complete conversion of life. Becoming a monk should be one of the most radical things a man could do with his life, for a monk's constant commitment is to changing himself to the very roots of his being. This total conversion is for a distinct purpose, to remove everything that would stand in the way of his dedication to God.

But it is a little more complicated than that, for the monk should be concerned, not only with changing himself, but, in a sense, with getting rid of himself. Merton assumes that when a man comes to a monastery he is still saddled with what he called the "empirical self," that is, an illusory idea rather than an existential reality. The "empirical self" is a façade, a shoddy conception of ourselves, rank in its artificiality, which, for whatever variety of reasons, we have built up in order to hide our true selves. Our true self, then, the person whom God intends us to be, is to be found behind the facade of the empirical self, and it is the duty of the monk to try to break down that facade and come to terms with his true self. It is by no means an easy task, and Merton made no attempt to suggest otherwise. The monk's life must, essentially, be one of abnegation. He must be prepared to declare ruthless war on his false self so that his true self can emerge victorious. In not at all a superficial way, the monk must be willing to suffer a kind of death, dying to his old self so that his new self might be born. Lest this sound too fantastic in tone, it could be pointed out that the monk is simply taking with the utmost seriousness one of the basic tenets of Christian belief: that if a man wants to gain his life, he must be prepared to lose it.

The monk's quest does not end, however, with the discovery of his true self; this is only the preliminary to that toward which his entire life and energies must incessantly be directed—union with God. We saw that the monk's true self was the self which God, from all eternity, destined him to be. By coming to terms with his true self, far from arriving at a kind of psychological dead-end, he in fact comes in contact with the infinite, for it is in the center of his being, having once discovered who he really is, that the monk discovers God. It is as if, in a manner of speaking, he does not stop at the discovered self but goes right on through it—the only route he could have taken, however—to meet something infinitely more interesting, the awful presence of the eternal Lord. The ultimate and paradoxical purpose of the monk's concern with himself is that he might become selfless. He seeks to find his true self so that he can forget about it, and lose himself in the eternal reality of God.

Having thus acquainted ourselves with what Merton considered the core identifying qualities of the monk—*metanoia* and union with God—we might imagine that any monk who succeeded in these most difficult accomplishments would be a decidedly distant and impotent fellow, someone who walked around from dawn to dusk in a state of spacey self-absorption, completely unaware of what was going on or, if aware, completely incapable of doing anything about it. Merton would totally reject this figment of our imagination. A man who has found his true self, and thus God, is one who, if anything, is more rather than less involved in the world about him. The difference is not between action and non-action, but between kinds of motivation for action. The man who has not found his true self acts in accordance with his own, often enfeebled, conceptions of what has to be done. The man in possession of his true self, however, acts in accordance with the divine light that burns within him. If not at all times infallible in what he does, he at least stands considerably less chance of going completely off the falls and acting foolishly. It cannot be expected, though, that the majority of monks will attain the state after which they aspire. There is no fixed schedule for the discovery of one's true self. For some it is a long process; for others—and the reason for this is hidden in the mystery of God—it is simply something not to be accomplished within the confines of this life at all. Whatever be the case, all monks must take a definite, conscious stance toward the world in which they live. That stance is in a sense taken by them as soon as they enter the monastery, for Merton believed that one of the essential characteristics of the monastic life was that it was a life of protest, protest against a world which is considered fundamentally wrong-headed in its commitment to things which are well calculated to do everything but lead a person to a discovery of his true self. The world, which, concretely, meant for Merton American society and culture, with its totally materialistic orientation, provided every possible barrier to prevent a person's ever coming into contact with his true self. In fact, the average person in the world was not even aware of the falsity of his identity. He could easily move through seventy years from birth to death and never once have experienced the exquisite pleasure of being really alive.

It was the monk's function, by leading a life dramatically contrary to such pseudo-life, to protest, to stand in judgment upon the world. For him to be at all effective in this, separateness was critical. He was making the best possible contribution to his society by not becoming lost in it. He must, in other words, maintain his identity as a monk. To emphasize the importance of this, Merton once remarked that "the monk, as such, is actually of no interest to anybody except insofar as he is really a monk." For this reason he had little patience with those who tried to tell him that monasticism was an anachronism, or, worse, that it was irrelevant. Most such criticism came from people who attached primary importance to social action, but Merton had seen enough, and been engaged enough in, social action to realize that some of it was precipitious and some disastrous. It was very important not to allow action to degenerate into mindless activism—action just for the sake of action—which happened much too often. At any rate, the supreme relevance of monasticism lay in the fact of its being consciously and determinedly irrelevant, that is to say, in its decision not to feel bound to keep up with what the world considers important, and more, continually to call into serious question, by its very existence, the value system of the world.

Merton was well aware that this *raison d'etre* of monasticism was completely unacceptable to many people. He knew that some, who were fairly close to him and whom he respected, thought that he was wasting his time and his talents by living in a monastery and not doing all he could be doing to make this world a better place in which to live. He was personally sorry that they saw things this way, but he did not agree with them for a moment. Ultimately one must face the paradoxical nature of the monastic life. A monk leaves the world for the sake of the world. He stands in judgment of that world not to damn it but to save it. He separates himself from men not to alienate himself from them but rather to seek a condition in which he can discover God, and discovering God and loving him he discovers all mankind and loves them in a way he could never have done before.

There were times, toward the end of his life, when he thought that much more important than explaining what it was to be a monk, or apologizing for being a monk, was the need simply to *be* a monk. Merton did a lot of explaining and very little apologizing. He spent twenty-seven years of his life in the earnest effort of being the best monk he knew how to be. His life in the monastery had its ups and downs. There were some aspects of monasticism which clearly bothered him and, as we saw, he did not hesitate to criticize them. But it is quite evident that this criticism sprang from love. It is impossible to believe, reading the works of Thomas Merton, that one is listening to an unhappy man. Quite the contrary, Merton evidences the contentment common to the man who knows the most important decision of his life was the right one, who writes from home. He fell in love with monasticism the first time he visited the Abbey of Gethsemani, in the spring of 1941, and the affair lasted for the rest of his life. It is not insignificant that the last talk he gave in his life, just a few hours before he died, was on monasticism.

CHAPTER V

THE WORLD AND ITS PROBLEMS

THE WORLD MAY BE too much with us, as Wordsworth once observed, but no matter how deep our antipathy for it nor how strong our desire to keep distant from it, we can never, short of being dead, reach the point where we are completely beyond its influence. This, as Thomas Merton was to learn, is as true for monks as it is for anybody else. At first, as we have seen, he did not think so. In his early years as a monk he was pretty firm in the conviction that he had completely severed his ties with the world outside the monastery walls. But this conviction was short-lived. On the practical plane, his becoming involved in large-scale publishing brought him, willy-nilly, into the turmoil and trauma of the American market place. A "famous author" cannot long remain a recluse, no matter to how strictly cloistered order he might belong, and shortly after *The Seven Storey Mountain* made Merton a personage as well known as Bishop Sheen and Father Keller, a stream of mail began flowing toward Trappist, Kentucky which was to continue steadily until the end of his life. Ideologically speaking, Merton was gradually going to come to the conclusion that the monk, even if he could completely separate himself from the world, should not do so. Physical separation, yes, for a monk is a monk only insofar as he lives a life which is clearly distinct from mankind at large, but spiritual separation never. The monk must realize that he is implicated in and responsible for his society. Just as it influences him he must strive, within

58

the bounds of his monastic vocation, to influence it, hopefully to change it for the good.

This awareness of a sense of responsibility toward society was not something which appeared only late in Merton's life. An openness to the world, a concern for its problems, had been a part of him since he had reached adulthood. It was a part which never had exclusive domination over his actions, however, for it had to contend continually with the Romantic poet, that part which eschewed the world and longed for the desert places. These two "Mertons" lived side by side within the one man throughout his life; at one time one would gain the ascendancy and become the dominant force that shaped his life, at another time, the other. If we pay attention to the times of intense influence of one or the other persona, we can detect the emergence of a simple but interesting pattern. Let us describe Merton's concern for and involvement in the world as his this-worldly attitude, and call the responses of the Romantic poet in him his other worldly attitude. Provided with these labels, we can say that while he was a student at Columbia a this-worldly attitude dominated. After his conversion to Catholicism and for his early years as a monk he was guided primarily by an other-worldly attitude. Finally, from about the mid-1950s to the end of his life a this-worldly attitude had assumed dominance once again.

This pattern, especially the second and third stages of it, provides a helpful context within which to understand better Merton's thought and writing, but it would be wrong to think of it as something rigid and uncompromising. We are, after all, dealing here with someone who lived and breathed and thought—which is to say, who was changing and complex—and any large generalization we make of him should not lose sight of this simple truth.

The first stage of the pattern, the this-worldliness which characterized Merton's undergraduate days at Columbia, was understandably not marked by a great deal of maturity. It was no less earnest for that, however. His flirtation with Communism, though having something of the faddish about it—it was not terribly unusual for an American college student of the thirties to be involved in one way or another with the Party—was inspired at bottom by an open-eyed awareness of the moral bankruptcy of European civilization and a sincere belief that Marxism was the wave of the future, a wave which would sweep away all corruption and wash all things clean. His enthusiasm for the millennial promise of Marxism did not last too long. As was the case with many who rallied around Communism during the thirties, what most drew them to the doctrine was its then adamant opposition to war. Merton, whose deep antipathy for war was one of the golden constants of his life, was particularly attracted by this aspect of the movement. But, as was also the case with many fellow travellers then, he became bitterly disillusioned when, through the Spanish Civil War, it became evident that for the sake of expediency the Party could easily put aside its anti-war stance. It turned out to be a very pliable point of view. What remaining faith he might have retained in Communism as a peace-oriented political system was completely crushed a few years later as a result of the pact signed by Hitler and Stalin. Despite his repudiation of the Party, however, Merton never abandoned a respect and admiration for many of the tenets of Marxist philosophy, which he had begun reading as a high school student. He realized that there was much in Marx which was sound, accurate, and eminently applicable to a Christian context. Toward the end of his life he was particularly interested in the relationships between Marxism and monasticism.

When Merton adopted a distinctly other-worldly attitude after his conversion and entrance into the monastery, it was in good part because of his discouragement over the state of the world at that time. His *Secular Journal* (written in the late thirties and early forties but published in 1959) emphatically demonstrates, for example, how deeply disillusioned and depressed he was as the inevitability of the Second World War became more and more apparent. One might be tempted to argue that it was this discouragement which precipitated his conversion and, eventually, his decision to become a monk, with the intention of suggesting that these were desperate measures which he took to escape from a world he could no longer cope with. But it would be difficult to find much evidence for this argument, for although Merton certainly "despaired" of the world—that is, he lost faith in men's ability to save themselves—he never showed the least bit of fear of it. He decried the coming war, for example, but was willing, as a Noncombatant Objector, to risk his life helping the wounded on the battlefield. Certainly, his sour attitude toward his society was a factor to be considered in discussing his decision to leave that society for one which was dramatically different from it, but it was not the most important factor, which was simply his desire to follow the evangelical counsels and seek perfection. In the final analysis we must conclude that Merton was not so much running away from something as he was running toward something. There was much more of the positive than the negative in his decision to become a monk.

There is no doubt, however, that for about his first fifteen years as a monk, he took a decidedly indifferent attitude toward the world he had left. His emphasis, as easily detected in his writings, was on personal sanctification and salvation. Individual weaknesses and evils were what he emphasized; those of society at large he virtually ignored. This is not to say that he had entirely forgotten society, or that he felt he had no obligation whatever toward it. Indeed he regarded as one of the crucial functions of the monk the duty to pray and do penance for the sins of mankind, to make reparation for the evils of the world and pray God that they might be overcome. But the responsibilities of the monk toward the world were seen to be primarily spiritual; his dealings with it were by indirection.

This attitude began to show signs of changing in the mid-1950s. In his book *No Man is an Island*, for example, published in 1955, we see him stressing the idea that love, to be true, must be a dynamically inclusive reality. A person does not love God in blissful isolation, but in union with the whole of mankind. It is the communal or social aspect of that love which lends it its essential strength and validity, and it is through that aspect that one is inspired by a deep sense of responsibility for his fellow man. As time passed Merton moved from simply a theoretical acknowledgment of the need for Christians to become actively engaged in the social and political life about them to himself becoming involved in concrete social issues of his day. This manifested itself most emphatically in the sixties, the last decade of his life. Of the books published during that period, most dealt in whole or in part with the Christian's life in and obligations toward the world. The theme was clear: if the Christian was ever justified in turning his back on the chaos of his time, he could now no longer do so in good conscience. He must confront the chaos head-on and do what he could to ameliorate it.

If the pattern is thus made complete by Merton assuming once again a this-wordly attitude, we must not simplistically think that it was anything like the attitude he displayed during his Columbia days. It differed fundamentally from that by reason of its sound theological base. When Merton called men, and especially Christians, to commit themselves to social revolution, it was not, as was the case when he was under the influence of Communism, in the belief that the human race could pull itself up by its own bootstraps. To the contrary, the world was going to be changed for the better only to the degree that men recognized their utter dependence upon God. In other words, they were to follow the pattern of praying as if everything depended upon Him and yet acting as if everything depended upon themselves. And another point which bears repeating is that Merton's new this-worldliness was not posited upon a more sanguine attitude toward contemporary society. If anything, he thought less of it—as it stood—than he ever had before, but it was precisely his low estimate of the status quo, and his acute awareness of the dangers inherent in it, which contributed toward his forming a new sense of responsibility toward it.

That is one reason, at least, which explains why Merton saw fit to become involved, mainly through his writing on specific social issues. There are at least two others, both of significant importance, which are worth mentioning. In a book published in 1960 called *Disputed Questions,* Merton included a fine critical essay on the Russian novelist and Nobel Prize winner Boris Pasternak, who had some years before initiated correspondence with him. The essay clearly displays the warm friendship Merton had felt for Pasternak, as well as his profound appreciation and respect for his art. But there is something else besides. The more Merton talks about the difficulties to which Pasternak was subjected as a direct result of the society in which he lived, and the way he bravely held to his beliefs and preserved his integrity despite those difficulties, the more it becomes apparent that Merton felt a deep affinity for Pasternak precisely for these reasons. I think that his meditations on the plight of Pasternak, as well as those of people similar to him (those of Father Alfred Delp and Franz Jagerstatter, for example) awoke in Merton a certain feeling of guilt at the fact that the society in which he was living might in many respects be as evil as the societies of those men, and yet, unlike them, he was not protesting against the evil. What I am saying is that the men whom Merton seemed to admire most toward the end of his life were distinguished for their open refusal to participate in the corruption which they saw around them, and he was influenced by them in that he too chose to adopt a stance of declared non-participation.

Another important causative factor behind Merton's awakened social consciousness is connected with his habit of drawing historical analogies, however carelessly at times. Specifically, Merton began, probably in the late fifties, to become very interested in the Germany of the 1930s. The subject had more than merely a theoretical appeal to him because he had, as a student, traveled extensively and spent a considerable amount of time in Germany during the early thirties, right after Hitler had come to power and while the country was being transformed into a Nazi nightmare. As Merton increased his knowledge of that phenomenon he was eventually led to the conclusion that there were some marked similarities between the Germany of the thirties and the United States of the sixties, and that it was not at all preposterous to suppose that something very much like what happened there could happen here. Far-fetched though the proposition may sound, it was undoubtedly sincerely held by Merton (as indeed it was by others at the time), and, at any rate, the point to be stressed is that Merton was concerned with averting a disaster and not smugly standing by to witness a prediction materialize and then having the dubious satisfaction of later claiming, among the debris and settling dust, that he had told us so. Merton was particularly disturbed by the guilt by complicity which the Catholic Church of Germany had brought down upon itself by not sufficiently speaking out against the blatant immoralities of Nazism. It is no good, he claimed, to say it is not the province of the Church to become involved in politics when non-involvement implies giving tacit approval to the most heinous kinds of crimes. In such a case not casting a ballot is interpretable as a vote for. But he was more sensitive yet toward the silence of the German monks in this situation, and it was their silence—with but few exceptions—which convinced him that there must be definite limits to the unworldly stance taken by monasticism. There comes a time, he decided, when the evil of a society is so great that the monk, in order to fulfill his vocation as one totally dedicated to God, must speak out against that evil, even if he does so in jeopardy of his life. It would be the grossest kind of irreligion if he neglected that duty with the excuse that his chief business was simply to work and pray within his monastery. Neither his work nor his prayer would ascend to God if, while he engaged in them, his brother, whose plight he deemed it expedient to ignore, was being murdered. It was because Merton felt that he was living in a society in many ways comparable to that of Germany in the thirities, that he made a special resolve, and kept it, not to imitate the peccable silence of those monks who calmly went about their daily routines while Hitler was in the process of building his hell.

There were two issues which he felt were critical to his

times, war and race, and it was to these that he devoted most of his attention. Needless to say, it did not require an over-powering amount of perceptivity, given the realities of the 1960s, to come to this conclusion, but Merton was doing more than simply deferring to the prevailing climate of opinion. Unlike many liberal intellectuals who during the sixties awoke for the first time in their lives to the realities that war is wasteful and absurd, and that American blacks are forced to live less than fully human lives, Merton was simply bringing out into the open—shouting from the housetops, one might say—what were old truths to him. We have already seen that he had consistently maintained an anti-war mentality throughout his adult life. As a Columbia undergraduate, for example, he took the Oxford Pledge never to participate in any war. After his conversion he acquainted himself with the Christian "just war theory" which, he was later to explain, traces itself back to St. Augustine. Nevertheless, he found great difficulty in reconciling himself to the rightness of American involvment in World War Two. No doubt Pearl Harbor altered his opinion, but not even that war, which was fairly clear-cut in its justifications for the majority of Americans, was without its serious questions for him. It is fairly easy, looking at the immediate causes of the outbreak of the fighting, both in Europe and in the Pacific, to claim that the United States and her allies were fully justified, according to Christian principles, in going to war, but this glibly ignores the long-range causes which led up to those immediate causes and in which the allies were implicated as well as the axis. Merton, who was never satisfied with superficial or first line explanations, could not ignore those long-range causes and consequently would not allow himself to be caught up in the fervor that regarded the war as being between the shining soldiers of light and the diabolic denizens of darkness. The Nazis and their cause were unquestionably evil, there was no doubt about that, but there was also no doubt, for him, that the allies were also tainted with sin. They had contributed, both actively and passively, to the growth of evil in the world. Their attitude of offended innocence, then, once that evil reached the bursting point and overflowed upon them, was singularly disingenuous and unconvincing.

It was the large and disturbing fact of the Vietnam war, more than anything else, which served as the chief impetus for Merton's speculations upon the Christian philosophy of war. Although he made several attempts to deal with the subject, he never ended with a tightly constructed, completely developed theory. This is not to say, however, that certain general views of his are not easily discernible. In the first place, he felt that something had gone seriously wrong with the primitive Christian ideal—that is to say, pre-fourth century—which was profoundly anti-violent and anti-war. He points out that the first Christians were prohibited from joining the Roman army or in anyway engaging in warfare. This tradition, which Merton obviously approved of and looked back upon with nostalgia, was doomed once the church became closely associated with civil powers, as it did after the reign of Emperor Constantine I. The church thus became part of the political establishment and her safety and welfare was thenceforth, and with dire consequences, linked with the safety and welfare of the establishment. From that time on Christians were forced to justify their participation in wars. St. Augustine was among the first to do this, although he tried to abide as much as he could by the law of charity, and he allowed war only as a means of self-defense. Even when engaged in war, he taught, Christians should not cease to love their enemies. Merton's attitude toward St. Augustine on this particular matter is ambivalent. On the one hand he could appreciate that St. Augustine was very much in a trying situation. The Roman empire was being overrun by invaders. Christian villages were being attacked, ransacked and burned. What were Christians to do in such circumstances, simply stand by and allow themselves to be cut down, while their wives and children were carried off as slaves? St. Augustine, understandably and with good cause, argued no. A Christian can in good conscience go to war to defend himself and his loved ones. On the other hand, although Merton could personally empathize with St. Augustine, given the situation with which he was faced, and although he could not logically refute his position, he felt that the Bishop of Hippo had been unwittingly instrumental in diverting Christianity away from one of its most precious traditions. In subsequent centuries Augustine's doctrine was going to be rudely seized upon by cynical rationalizers and twisted to the point where it was virtually unrecognizable, with the end result that Christians would soon begin to justify their participation in any and all kinds of war, not the least of which were those waged against fellow Christians.

Despite his deep-set dissatisfaction with the way the Christian philosophy of war had developed, despite his own constitutional opposition to war, Merton could never bring himself to admit that all war, *per se*, was immoral. Given the unfortunate but undeniable realities of human relationships, there were going to be times when one people would launch an unprovoked attack on another, and in such instances the attacked were fully justified in defending themselves. But that was it. Only wars of self-defense were justifiable according to Christian doctrine and this rendered a war like that in Vietnam, except by the most perverse kind of casuistry, totally indefensible. Merton made it poignantly explicit more than once that he considered that war to be unqualifiedly immoral; it was the low point in American history. Even though he could theoretically allow for a defensive war, he asked if, with the practical realities of the world situation being what they are, it made sense to condone "limited" war when it could so easily explode into a global confrontation in which the very existence of the human race would be at stake. He did not hesitate to condemn the unlimited use of nuclear weapons as being in any and all cases immoral.

There were two interesting repercussions to Merton's outspokenness on the subject of war in general and to his specific attacks against the United States' involvement in Vietnam. In the first place he was subjected to censorship by his monastic superiors, who felt, apparently at the suggestion of higher ecclesiastical authorities in this country, that it was not his province to speak out on matters which properly the theologians should be dealing with. Although he submitted to the decision of his superiors, he was deeply disturbed by an action which he considered logically indefensible. He would have been more than willing to concede the podium to the theologians; the only trouble was that the theologians were conspicuous for their non-committal attitude. They were saying nothing, while in the meantime the country, because of the war, seemed to be on the brink of utter chaos. Was one to maintain silence in the face of such a situation? Merton thought not. The censorship, though painful and discouraging, was temporary. No doubt because eventually many officials in the Catholic Church in the United States began themselves to have serious qualms about the war—this in turn probably brought about by the new atmosphere created by the Second Vatican Council—the pressures on Merton began to ease. By the last few years of his life he was free to write whatever he wanted on the subject of war.

Another result of his anti-war attitude was that many Catholics, especially those who had admired, even idolized, the early Merton, became disillusioned with him. This phenomenon was dramatically illustrated by an incident which took place in 1967 when Merton publicly supported a Catholic college student who refused to submit to induction because of his conviction that the Vietnam war was unjustifiable. The story of Merton's action was run in the Catholic newspaper of the diocese of Louisville. The news brought heated response from the readers over the next five weeks, most of it decidedly anti-Merton. The gist of the criticism was that Merton, by his becoming involved in what was essentially a political issue, was being disloyal to his contemplative vocation. One reader tried to prove that Merton was an incompetent philosopher. Another lamented the fact that the monk was tragically incapable of appreciating that the war in Vietnam was a to-the-death struggle with godless Communism. Such criticism hurt Merton, for he took no special joy in alienating himself from anyone, but it did not sway him from the conviction that he was right and his critics were wrong. He had already reached the conclusion that a good number of those who were shocked and scandalized by his concern for social issues were what he pejoratively designated as "good Catholics," that is, Christians in whose lives one detects little or no practical manifestation of the faith they profess. Religion, in other words, really did not make a difference in their lives.

As was the case with his attitude toward war, Merton's thoughts on the subject of race had been part of his general world view for many years. It is instructive to recall in this context that his decision to become a monk was the alternative to his joining Catherine de Hueck Doherety and her work in Harlem. He had already helped out for short periods at her Friendship House there and the experience made a deep and lasting impression upon him. Reading the journal entries he made at the time, one is struck by the depth and sincerity of his empathy for the inhabitants of New York's ghetto, as well as by the poignancy of his analysis of the black American experience in general. He was over twenty years ahead of his time in making observations of which the vast majority of his white contemporaries were incapable, but which were to become the truisms of the civil rights movement of the sixties. So impressed was Eldridge Cleaver with the moving descriptions of the dreary and dehumanizing life of Harlem to be found in *The Seven Storey Mountain* that, as he recounts in *Soul on Ice*, he copied them out long hand and used to refer to them when giving Black Muslim lectures.

Merton gave unqualified support to the black revolution which followed the civil rights movement. Although he had no immediate knowledge of the various psychological and sociological changes that were taking place for many blacks, he displayed an uncanny ability to read correctly a complex and quickly evolving situation. In a book published in 1964, *Seeds of Destruction*, he estimated that a point of no return had been reached. The suppressed rage of American blacks, the result of their being consistently deprived of full participation in the national life, was soon to burst into violent protest. He predicted that within the next few years blacks would begin to flow out of their ghettoes across the country

and wreak destruction upon contiguous white neighbor-
hoods; their special targets would be the white businesses, the
chief symbols for them of an affluent way of life which was
always tantalizingly proximate but in which they could never
adequately share. There were some who thought he was being
altogether too pessimistic in his prediction and chided him
for being a simplistic alarmist. Although he proved to be
wrong in thinking that the destructiveness would take place
outside the ghetto rather than inside it, subsequent events,
especially the explosive summer of 1967, demonstrated his
analysis and prediction to be in the main quite accurate. It
was not the first time in his life that his penchant for brush-
ing past surface complexities and his intuitive ability to get
right to the heart of the matter had served him very well.

It is in his social thought more than in anything else that
one is made aware of the close affinity between Merton and
the times in which he lived. As is the case with every thinker
of significance, he was influenced by his age—by the prevailing climates of opinon, ideologies and intellectual fads—as
well as he influenced it. Without belaboring the obvious, one
can call attention to the fact that the pattern of his attitudes
toward society, discussed above, reflects opinions which, respectively, held sway within American culture at the time. If
he was dynamically this-worldly and concerned with social
problems as a Columbia student during the thirties it was at
least in part because social concern was very much in the air
during that era. So too, the withdrawn other-worldliness
which characterized the Merton of the forties and most of
the fifties finds its reflection in the general mood of the
country at that time. Finally, it is quite obvious that he was
far from being alone when, during the sixties, he awakened to
a new social consciousness. This was a decade when many
intellectuals left their ivory towers and churchmen their
cloisters to become earnestly, if not always intelligently,
engaged in a society which previously they had pretty much
ignored. In this respect, then, Thomas Merton, for all his
seclusion in the hills of Kentucky, was very much a man of
his times. The prevailing winds reached him there, and he was

affected by them. At the same time, not to forget the other side of the coin, some significant winds blew out of the hills of Kentucky and had their effect on the rest of the country.

Given the amount he wrote on social issues during the last ten or so years of his life, it is imperative, if anything like a complete picture of Merton is to be arrived at, that he be considered and assessed in his capacity as a social critic. I will begin by suggesting that his best talents did not lie in this area. He lacked the patience and prosaic persistence to examine minutely the many ramifications of the various matters he wrote about, with the result that his analyses were not always accurate nor his judgments sound. He was really more of a prophet than he was a social critic, which is by no means to put him in a lesser category. I use the term prophet in the same sense in which he applied it to himself, that is, as designating not so much a predictor of the future as a discerning instinctive reader of the present. However, as was evidenced in what he had to say about the racial situation in this country, he certainly was not bereft of predicting abilities and therefore can, to a limited degree, be considered a prophet in that sense as well. The instinctive approach he took toward the analysis of social problems seemed to produce extreme results. Either he was right on the mark, as in his seeing the inevitability of wide-spread rioting of black Americans three years before it took place, or he was off target completely, as when he suggested, in 1962, that De Gaulle might be assassinated and that the United States was in imminent danger of becoming a fascist state.

Perhaps the single most important factor contributing toward blurring his vision of the social scene was his pessimism, which will be discussed at some length in a chapter to follow. And the specific error most often produced by his pessimism was over-simplification. Perhaps this tendency to be simplistic can also be attributed to his philisophico-theological background, which had trained him to break down issues into sometimes too neat categories and, in terms of ethics, too readily to reduce complex matters to a simple dichotomy of good and evil. In the matter of the Vietnam war, for example, there is evidence that this sad phenomenon was brought about, as he argued, by the semidiabolical machinations of cynical, power-hungry ogres and/or of misguided, questionably sane fanatics, but not, as he also suggested, exclusively so. Merton sometimes found it difficult to believe in the sincerity, and often the sanity, of those who did things with which he did not agree; and it is helpful to know that throughout his life he maintained a deep distrust for politicians. Along with "businessman," "politician" was one of the bad words in his vocabulary. It was very hard for him, therefore, to accept the fact that some of those leaders who were directly responsible for American involvement in Vietnam sported no horns and trailed no tail, neither did they carry a barbed pitch fork in their hands. But the sometimes simplistic way he looked at the war can also be traced to another attitude which was central to his world view. This attitude is best illustrated by something he once said, in an unpublished book entitled *Peace in a Post-Christian Era*: "We have to face the fact that war is not merely the product of blind political forces, but of human choices, and if we are moving closer and closer to war, this is because that is what men are freely choosing to do." There is something cleanly refreshing and admirable in this unapologetic and forthright declaration of the strategic importance of human choice. This is a theme Merton sounded again and again, and with good cause. However, while not denying for a moment that what eventuates in the affairs of men is chiefly the result of what men chose to do, it must also be recognized that events sometimes get the better of men. They may have been precipitated by clear-cut and easily identifiable choices, but once they grow and gain momentum they often take on a life of their own and can even reach the point where they control men rather than men control them. This idea, in its general outline, was by no means strange to Merton, and in fact he applied it often when discussing the technological aspects of modern life: technological man creates a machine which he ends up being controlled by rather than controlling, hence he himself becomes a machine. Strangely, though, he never thought to apply the idea to the Vietnam war, a phenomenon to which, or so at least it seems to me, it is eminently applicable. Here was a case where, by whatever combination of initial deciding, conniving or bungling—and the more one reads about the "causes" of the war the more one despairs of ever sorting it all out, a monster was quickly created who overpowered and made a slave out of the master. In a sense, then, the Vietnam war was some-something that happened to America rather than, as Merton wanted to think, something which was carefully mapped out at the outset by ruthless men at the top. While too many people were looking the other way it burgeoned into a major crisis, and when they turned around they felt they had no choice but to declare themselves either four-square behind American involvement or adamantly against it. At any rate, it was something which developed in many respects independently of men's choices rather than on account of them.

One detects Merton's weakness for simplistic analysis in some of the things he had to say about the racial situation as well. This showed itself in two ways. First, he had a tendency to blame the sad plight of black Americans not just on the white man but specifically on the white liberal, the one who, presumably, was very conscious of that plight and anxious to do something about it. He accused the white liberal, in essence, of being a phony; his concern for the black man was simply a part of his felt need to live up to the role which he thought proper to him. It was a purely theoretical concern, and was incapable of manifesting itself in the kinds of practical ways which, when the chips were down, were really going to count. For example, the white liberal was all for the black gaining his full dignity as a person and his rights as a citizen so long as he did not move in next door. Besides being cruelly harsh, this assessment is severely distorted, doing considerably less than justice to those many white liberals who were willing to, and in fact did, put their lives on the line for what they believed. But it is also a rather puzzling position to take for one who himself was a white liberal. If what he said about the lack of sincerity in the group was true, the tables could easily be turned on him by calling into question the stability of what he himself had to say on this subject. Merton had a way of exaggerating, and distorting, to make a point, not out of malice, however, but out of the passion with which he held certain views. No doubt it was the intensity of his feeling for the suffering of his black fellow citizens that made him too quick in putting so much of the blame for that suffering on the white liberals. Perhaps his own feeling of guilt was a causative ingredient. It is pretty certain that another was the credulous, uncritical ear he gave to what many black radicals had to say on the subject.

The second major way in which he slipped into the simplistic on the racial question—and this too, I think, was largely attributable to his habit of believing implicitly whatever the black radical had to say—was his reluctance to acknowledge that there was anything at all wrong with the actions certain blacks were taking to remedy their situation. What this boiled down to was his reluctance to condemn the use of violence. This is all the more unexpected because, by and large, Merton was repulsed by violence and saw it as essentially absurd because ultimately self-defeating. There is a disconcerting inconsistency, therefore, in his unwillingness to point out that violence as a solution to one's problems, personal or social, will prove to be as much a blind alley for American blacks as it has been for everyone else since time immemorial. He came dangerously close to making the kind of self-serving, facile distinction which he consistently repudiated in other contexts, that distinction which separates "your" violence, which is bad, from "my" violence, which is good. In this case the violence of blacks could be winked at because it was justified; but this fails to recognize that practically all large-scale violence in the course of human history has been justified (that is, rationalized) and therein lies the problem not the solution.

One of the most disarming qualities of this simplistic element in Merton's social criticism is that it is not seldom admixed with some acute and quite accurate observations. He has, for example, some perceptive and I think appropriate things to say about the mass media. In general he had little confidence in them. He held the theory that very little "news" is what we are led to believe it is. It is not something, in other words, which happens independently of the mass media and which the mass media then dutifully reports. On the contrary, most of what we call "news" is the fabrication or the manipulated result of the mass media. There are very few true reporters; most of them are simply, in Merton's special use of the term, newsmakers. This idea may not be entirely original with him, but he elaborates upon it in very clever and engaging ways, making applications of it which are singularly convincing. It definitely contributes to a more balanced view of the media in this country. But, juxtaposed to such contributions are sweeping judgments of those media which simply will not hold water. For example, he could not divest himself of the idea that the mass media was in con-spiratorial cahoots with the governmental establishment and consequently the insidious means by which the citizenry was kept in its impotent place and brain-washed into accepting the establishment line on every important issue. This analysis ignores what was probably the biggest instance in American history of the mass media and the governmental establish-ment being at loggerheads. I refer to the fact that during the 1960s the most trenchant and persistent opposition to the Vietnam war emanated from the mass media, and there is no doubt that the gradual widespread disillusionment with the government-backed war among the American people was due primarily to media opposition. Be that as it may, one of the ironies of Merton's generally caustic regard of the mass media is that he himself was so thoroughly affected by them in so many ways, besides being, in no mean manner, a part of them. On the one hand the number of books he published made him a major contributor to the mass media. On the other, had it not been for the medium of books he would have been without the vast complex of ideas and attitudes which played so important a part in his life and which, in-deed, in great part made him what he was.

It is often when he detaches himself from specific issues

and considers the world exclusively in terms of general theories that one is provided with the most poignant examples of his over-simplication. Throughout his writings one finds several metaphoric attempts to reduce complex situations to the simplest possible terms. "Gog" becomes the symbol for the West, looked upon as a monolith, and "Magog" the symbol for the East, also seen as a huge, undifferentiated politico-social mass. In another case he makes an attempt to divide the whole of humanity into three parts, designated respectively as "we," "they" and the "others." "We" are the concerned intellectuals, whose duty it is to protect "the others," the vast majority of mankind, the simple and unpretentious people, from the evil designs of "them," who are the ruthless and power-hungry politicians and militarists of the world. In such theorizing one perceives, besides the simplistic, also a tinge of supercilious elitism. The "we" seem too smugly right for comfort, too secure in their position of superiority vis-à-vis the two other groups. Perhaps this was the Romantic poet coming to the fore once again, inclining Merton to conceive of the "good guys" as sensitive and talented rebels who stood above the fray and upon whom the salvation of mankind ultimately depended. Too, if his conception of intellectuals is somewhat rough-hewn and perhaps a little naive, it might be explained by the fact that, because of his monastic seclusion, he was not in intimate contact for a large portion of his life with those who think of themselves as such. Although my opinion on this might be unfairly biased, it seems that wide and lengthy exposure to intellectuals is the surest preventative of ever thinking that there is something charismatically special about such people or that they alone hold the key to world peace and prosperity.

After it has been pointed out that Merton's social criticism suffers most from simplistic reasoning, the subject should not be closed without acknowledging that such reasoning was not entirely without its redeeming qualities. No matter how unbalanced the cumulative results of Merton's barging in upon a complex situation to come up with a simplistic analysis often proved to be, there was long-term benefit in what he did, for he was opening up issues which many refused to touch precisely because of their complexity. Indeed for some, especially intellectuals, referring to something as a "complex situation" was simply an evasive tactic, a means of avoiding an issue which one had neither the moral courage nor mental stamina to contend with. This seemed to be the case for some time with respect to the Vietnam war. Merton, very much in his capacity as prophet, waded in where angels feared to tread, and even though everything he had to say about a subject may not have been scientifically indisputable, he did succeed in calling attention to the vital importance of the subject. And for that he should not be faulted; for that he should be praised.

What must not be forgotten about Merton is that he was a thinker in the best sense of the term, which is to say, among other things, that he was constantly going over his own tracks; he was constantly reviewing his thoughts and rigorously testing them for stability and durability. One sees this most clearly in his various attitudes toward society and its problems. There is scarcely a conclusion he arrived at, a theory he established, which he did not come back to —often several times—to adjust and refurbish; sometimes he returned simply to demolish. He had no qualms whatever about changing his mind. Like Emerson, he refused to be bothered by charges of inconsistency. Merton, if not initially at least eventually, was as aware of the flaws in his thinking on social issues as was any critic. For example, it was no secret to him that he had a tendency to oversimplify, and, specifically, he came to recognize the limitations of opting for facile distinctions such as that he made among "we," "them" and "the others," and he warned his friends from falling into the same trap.

For all the one-sided, extremely-stated conclusions he showed himself to be capable of arriving at, he also possessed a built-in respect for tentativeness. Very rarely were any of his conclusions final. There was a strain of ambivalence likely to be found in even his most emphatically definitive pronouncements. This is explained, at bottom, by his basic common sense, which was always jealous to establish a solid relationship between what he said and what were the facts, and a humility which always kept his fallibility squarely in front of him and never allowed him to take his own ideas too seriously. Thoroughly committed to the truth, he knew that it was not something any one man could lay exclusive claim to. His respect for the mystery in which all human experience was immersed taught him that there was of necessity an element of the uncertain in the most certain of man's theories about society or about anything else. To admit less would be to renege on his overriding dedication to wisdom.

CHAPTER VI

THE WIDER VISION

IT IS DIFFICULT TO FIND a single stagnant moment in the whole of Thomas Merton's intellectual life. Mentally, he was always on the move. A man of irrepressible inquisitiveness, he was constantly engaged in expanding his intellectual horizons, seeking out and settling down in new territory, where he quickly became right at home and often began to assume the speech and mannerisms of a native.

Yet at the same time, side by side with the changing complexion and the incessant expansion of his thought, there was a certain permanence, a core of stability around which his diverse ideas revolved and from which they gained their focus and coherence. My stating the case in these terms reflects an image which Merton himself once used to describe his intellectual life. He said that his ideas were always changing, always moving around one center, always seeing that center from somewhere else. He did not go on to say what was the constituency of that "one center," but he hardly needed to have done so, for every aspect of his life clearly points it out. The "one center"—which held for him to the end—was a composite of the tenets of Christian theology and the traditions of monasticism. To these he gave his complete, though never passive, loyalty, and it was upon these that, literally to his dying day, he was constantly building or remodeling the structure of his thought with an amazing variety of ideas and ideologies. Given this variety, the structure in question took on a decidedly eclectic nature, which can be regarded as either a plus or a minus. One way or the other, it offers serious problems for the person who wants to identify the separate parts of which the whole is composed.

It will one day be the laborsome but fascinating task of a meticulous and dedicated scholar to isolate and identify the many influences which went together to form Merton's broad and scintillating world view. I certainly make no pretentions of accomplishing such a task in this chapter, but I do endeavor to discuss what to me are four major elements of that world view. They are Marxism, the philosophy of non-violence, existentialism, and oriental philosophy and religion. To return for a moment to the image proposed by Merton, these were, in my view, the largest satellites which revolved around the "one center" of his intellectual life.

Let us begin with Marxism. Though he never was what could be called a full-fledged Marxist thinker, Merton from the time he first began to read him as a high school student, continued to maintain a commitment to some of the basic premises of Marx's philosophy. What impressed him most about this philosophy was the intensely critical stance it took toward contemporary social structures. Given what appears to be his natural indisposition to the modern world, he was inevitably going to be appealed to by this aspect of Marxism. However, though he was not at all hesitant in pointing out serious and possibly even fatal defects in capitalism, he was not prepared to state definitively that the capitalistic system was intrinsically and irredeemably evil and that consequently it should be replaced. But one thing was clear: because of the gross injustices it embodied, it was not deserving of survival under its present form. Reform was absolutely necessary. Another trait of Marxism, or more exactly of certain Marxists, which Merton admired and in a sense emulated was a high and dedicated idealism. He was enamored by the fervor with which these people believed what they believed, and, more critically, the manner in which they patterned their lives after their beliefs. In this trait he felt that many Christians, by comparison, would be put to shame. Thirdly, Merton adopted from Marxism and employed extensively in his own thought the concept of alienation. With Marx, he believed that what chiefly distinguishes the man living today in Western, industrialized society is a vague but painful sense of being cut off from himself; he feels a stranger not only to his own deepest being, and thus is in constant search of his identity, but also to his environment, the world around him. Isolated, alone and afraid, he has more of the characteristics of an automaton than a man. Life has lost virtually all meaning for him. He lives constantly on the dull but irritating edge of desperation.

Finally, Merton borrowed and incorporated into his way of thinking the fundamental doctrine of Marxism, the dialectical approach to reality. He felt that, with modifications, the paradigm of thesis meeting antithesis to resolve itself in a synthesis was an instructive one, and could have wide and profitable applicability to many issues of today's world. For example, he thought that this dialectical approach could be of use to the Christian who was concerned with ecumenism. Faced with the reality of the many divisions now existent in Christianity, the Christian, Merton contended, should first learn to accept them, then work with them, and ultimately go beyond them.

If many of the tenets of Marxism can be found throughout Merton's thought, there is a way in which his decision to become a monk was a dramatic practical manifestation of the favoritism he displayed toward that ideology. One is reminded, in this context, of what he said in *Seeds of Contemplation*: "A man cannot be a perfect Christian—that is, a saint—unless he's also a communist." Merton's explicit and unapologized-for aim in life was to become a saint, and there is not doubt that he looked upon the monastic life as providing the kind of communistic community which he felt was most conducive to sanctity. A good monk was the truest kind of communist. While eschewing private property, he also abandoned all pursuits of an egocentric and self-serving nature; he was dedicated uncompromisingly to the community. This life-long affection to grassroots communism is also evidenced in the unusually strong nostalgia Merton at times displayed for primitive Christianity, where, as the Acts of the Apostles tells us, the brethren held all things in common.

But while we acknowledge the importance which Marxism and communistic ideals played in Merton's life and thought, we must also recognize the highly qualified way in which they did so. No one could have been more diametrically opposed to, for example, the materialistic orientation of Marxist thought than was Thomas Merton for him, what was most wrong with modern man was that, like Marx, he had accepted the material as the be-all and end-all of his life. In doing so he had led himself down a blind alley. So too, while Merton agreed with Marx's description of the alienated man, he in no wise accepted his program for dis-alienation. He made quite clear what he thought lay at the bottom of all social alienation; it was "man's alienation from the deepest truth, from the springs of spiritual life within himself, his alienation from God." Modern alienated man, then, according to Merton, was only going to overcome his alienation by acknowledging the ground and center of his being, which was God. By the same token, the communism by which Merton guided his life was definitely of the small "c" variety. He had no illusions whatever about the Communist party, which he felt attempted to extend its influence by crass, deceptive and dehumanizing means; in other words it demonstrated, in these respects, a great affinity to capitalism. When it came down to the realities of politics, as opposed to the fineries of ideology, he saw very little difference between East and West, Communist and Capitalist. It was six of one and half-dozen of the other.

When we consider Merton's interest in the philosophy of non-violence, which began to play a large part in his writings during the sixties, it is necessary to recall that this, as was true of so many other aspects of his thought, had been with him, at least in germ, for most of his adult life. Certainly his life-long antipathy for war was based from the outset on at least an unconscious conviction that violence is not a solution to human problems. Merton saw that violence, proposed as a solution, was in fact a non-solution; it did not break into the vicious circle of hatred, but only tightened that circle, made it more impenetrable. Love and love alone was capable of breaking into the circle of hatred and dissipating it altogether.

Unquestionably it was the seemingly endless proliferation of violence in the world in which he lived which spurred Merton to seek out philosophic support for his non-violent leanings. He was to find it in many places, primarily in the teachings of Christ. As his writings on the nonviolent and anti-war convictions of the early Christians demonstrate, he was himself convinced that the whole drift of Christ's teachings was unquestionably toward non-violence and that, therefore, one of the most important titles by which Christ should be honored and esteemed is the Prince of Peace. He also relied heavily on many of the Church fathers for the development of his ideas on non-violence. Among such fathers were Clement of Alexandria, Justin Martyr, St. Cyprian, Tertullian and Maximus the Confessor. Merton also owed a considerable amount to Albert Camus on this score. But the person upon whom he relied the most, and by whom he was most inspired, was Mohandas K. Gandhi.

What chiefly drew Merton to Gandhi, I think, was the essentially courageous nature of the Mahatma's nonviolent philosophy. Merton often took pains to point out that he was not a pacifist; though against war, he would not disallow the theoretical possibility that in certain extreme circumstances—to protect oneself from an unprovoked invasion, for example—war was an unavoidable expedient. More positively, he believed that peace is not brought about by passively acquiescing to the evils which exist in the world. Evil must be actively combatted, but not by violence, for the nature of evil is such that it can only be overcome by its opposite, goodness. The non-violence of Gandhi is a manifestation of goodness because, among other things, it starts by recognizing the basic goodness of all men, which is to say that it is based upon love rather than hatred. To act out of a motivation of love for one's fellow man, rather than out of hatred for him, is the most courageous thing a man can do; in fact the courage demanded here is heroic in its proportions. For this reason the truly non-violent man is the farthest thing from a coward, and the non-violent way the farthest thing from weakness.

Following Gandhi closely, Merton formulated a philosophy of non-violence which was decidedly unsentimental in tone. Harboring no illusions about the nature of evil or the imperfection of human nature, it was based solidly upon the truth, the truth about man's right relation to his fellow man, and that upon which all else rested, his relation to God. In other words, the non-violent man sought justice for himself and for others in the society in which he lived; he also sought the love of God and union with Him. The two, far from being incompatible, of necessity went hand in hand. The supreme test of the non-violent man's commitment to his ideals was his willingness to lay down his life for those ideals. He had to be willing, literally, to put his life on the line. Merton made it explicit that in this he adhered strictly to the Gandhian philosophy, pointing out that, as a monk, he could not in good conscience do physical harm to another man, even if it were a matter of protecting his own life.

Love lay at the core of Merton's non-violent philosophy. Love was the great simplifier. So many people, when asked to consider love-inspired non-violence as an alternative to self-perpetuating, self-defeating hatred, scoff at what they consider to be its naive, simplistic and unrealistic approach. Ah, they say, you do not understand. The situation is much more complicated than you think. Indeed it is, and they are right. Hatred is always complicated. Love, on the other hand, is always simple. Merton realized that it was only the divine simplicity of love which could overcome the debilitating complications of hatred. He realized that only when men succeed in conjuring up courage to love one another as the brothers which they are will their eyes be open and will they see the utter absurdity in the non-solution which is violence.

Existentialism is one of those realities which are easier to describe than define. The most influential philosophical movement of our times—as I suppose was true of every philosophical movement in its prime—defies a strict pinning down, not the least reason for which is that most of those who call themselves existentialists seem to find it difficult to get together on who they are and what they are doing. We would soon be apprised otherwise if we thought that Merton remedied the situation, that he came up with a succinct, lucid and coherent explication of existentialism. Even if he did attempt such a task, which he did not, it probably would not have been too successful, for the fact of the matter was, Merton did not score high marks as a systematic thinker. Which is not necessarily to denigrate him. Systematic thinkers are fine if they have something to systematize, otherwise they are deadly bores, usually talking about nothing with great precision and thoroughness. Merton, though he did not always order his thought with architectonic splendor, did have a lot of thought which could have been so ordered. And that, in the final analysis, makes all the difference. He was very much an eclectic thinker, which I imagine is abundantly clear by this point, and he can be called an existentialist—and he often called himself an existentialist—to the degree to which we find in his thought many of the elements normally associated with the existentialist movement.

As was the case with Marxism, Merton picked and chose from existentialism, taking those ideas which he considered intrinsically sound and—what was always the most important consideration for him—which were compatible with the basic Christian orientation of his thought, while he rejected the others. It is difficult to say what writer first turned him toward existentialism, although there is a strong likelihood that it was Albert Camus. Certainly Camus was one of his favorite people, and although he once emphatically declared that the French novelist was not an existentialist, he generally considered him as such, and he seems to have derived a good many of his existentialist ideas from him. He liked Camus' emphasis on personal integrity, for example, an integrity which was defined by a person's exercising his free choice to

attain to a fully human existence in the face of the depersonalizing forces of mass society. In other words, he liked Camus
because he was a humanist; he stood up for man in the face
of all the forces which were trying to crush him. Although he
demonstrated an awareness of the major figures in the development of existentialism, Kierkegaard, Heidegger and Sartre,
as well as a general familiarity with their thought, he does not
seem to have read them extensively. I make this admittedly
precarious judgment on the basis of what strikes me as his
superficial commentary on these men; Kierkegaard he tends
to treat too tenderly, and Sartre too harshly. Karl Jaspers and
Gabriel Marcel were two existentialist thinkers whom he
knew well and by whom he was apparently influenced considerably. Another writer who might be considered existentialist in tone and who influenced him was the Austrian Max
Picard. Theologians such as Rudolf Bultmann and Karl Barth,
often regarded as existentialists, also had a substantial effect
upon his thought. If we were to broaden the definitions of
the terms existentialism and existentialist to the point where
they become all-inclusive—as Merton was sometimes inclined
to do—then the list of those who influenced him becomes
well-nigh interminable. For example, he detected strains of
existentialism in philosophers like Jacques Maritain and
Etienne Gilson and in novelists like Flannery O'Connor—all
of whom he read extensively. Such an exercise would only
confuse an issue which already has more than its share of
confusion, however, and my intent here is to clarify.

Perhaps what most characterizes Merton as an existential
thinker, on the superficial level, is that like so many existentialists, he freely employs the jargon which is common to the
movement without bothering to explain what it means.
"Authenticity" is a case in point. For the existentialist anything which bears the label of "authentic" is good: "authentic choice," "authentic human situation," "authentic relationship." There is a vague sort of way, I suppose, in which
we all apprehend what is being indicated by these terms without it being spelled out for us; and it is this quasi-instinctive
apprehension which the existentialist is probably banking on

to insure that his meanings are being conveyed. But this is a chancy means of communication at best, for one can never be sure about the uniformity, or perhaps I should say communality, of such apprehensions. To be more explicit about it, how can one be sure that his conception of "authentic human situation," for example, is shared by others? "Human" is a wide and comprehensive word, and we know by experience that one man's humanness is often another man's inhumanness; and between these two extremes there is room for a dizzying number of variations on the theme. In fairness to Merton, it must be said that he did not indulge in this careless jargonizing to the point where it became a serious obstacle, and he often took care to explain what he meant when he used the jargon. It is none the less present in his writing, however, to distract and sometimes to irritate. Ironically, in this propensity of existentialists to jargonize, we find they are succumbing to something which philosophically they claimed they are against, abstraction and mystification.

On a deeper level, there were many important elements of his thought which, if he did not derive them directly from existentialist thinkers, are at least similar to certain ideas which figure strategically in the existentialist movement. Indeed, as he himself pointed out, existentialism so permeated the contemporary intellectual atmostphere that one did not have to read specific philosophers to become familiar with it. One came by it almost unconsciously, simply by being alive and intellectually curious. We have already had occasion, when discussing the Romantic poet in Merton, to call attention to the fact that there was always a bit of the rebel about him, and that the target of his rebelliousness was most often the social status quo. He very much liked to think of himself as an anti-establishment man. This trait, as well as being Romantic, is definitely existentialist (the overlap is not strange, for of course existentialism itself has in it much of the Romantic), and we recall that this was the hallmark of the father of the movement, Soren Kierkegaard. By the same token, we can see echoes of Merton's uncomfortableness with, and sometimes explicit antagonism toward, modern technology in writers like Jaspers and Marcel. There is little doubt that he gleaned many of the ideas with which he refined his anti-modern attitude from these two men, especially from Jaspers, but it is equally true that he came to these men with the attitude already a part of his world view, albeit in an embryonic state. More than once he admitted that he had nothing against technology as such. In itself it was good. It was the manner in which it was being used that was evil. And how was that? In such a way that man had lost control of the very machines he had created. He was no longer controlling them; they were controlling him. The tragic result of this situation was that man had been de-manned. He had been so thoroughly dehumanized that he himself was little more than a machine. If the contemporary social scene looked so bleak and depressing, it was because modern technological society was but a conglomerate of bloodless integers, automatons, interacting among one another. The scene could be changed only if men threw off the ideologies of positivism, scientism and sociologism (words used often by Merton to describe philosophies which regarded men as machines rather than persons) which lay behind the technological revolution. What especially attracted him to a novelist like Flannery O'Connor was the belief that in much of what she wrote she was repudiating the positivistic way of looking at man.

Apropos of Merton's repeated protestations that he did not regard technology as intrinsically evil, I often get the impression that there was less than total earnestness in what he said, not that intellectually he did not want to believe it but that emotionally he found himself incapable of doing so. Reading the many dire things he had to say about the gradual mechanization of the Abbey of Gethsemani, especially the farm, one concludes that there was a deep-set, perhaps irreversible, quality to the antagonism he felt toward technology. The machine, both as symbol and fact, represented a serious danger to man because it was a potential—it seems at times that he thought inevitable—cause of alienation, a separater of man from nature, and ultimately of man from himself. Merton, it seems to me, if given the choice between a machine and no machine, would personally have preferred no machine. In a way which is difficult to explain, it is better to have the wagon drawn by two mules than a tractor. One thing is sure, it is quieter that way and for a Trappist that is is not a mean consideration.

The concept of absurdity, an important element in existentialist doctrine, also played a considerable role in Merton's thought. At first glance, given his Christian beliefs, this might appear somewhat incongruous, perhaps a little scandalous. But a closer look tells otherwise. Certainly he did not subscribe to the declaration that life is absurd in the same way as would a Sartre, or even a Camus. Whereas an atheistic existentialist would claim that life was absurd through and through, Merton, as a Christian, maintained that the absurdity was more apparent than real, that is to say, it applied to surface realities rather than to what lay beneath them. Human life, the actions of men, no matter what disconcerting mysteries they may provide to fuel man's pain and frustration, are founded upon an infinite depth of meaning. That meaning, the Ground upon which they rest and from which they derive their existence, is the eternal reality of God. But to offer this explanation is not to alleviate the pain, or, if you will, the absurdity, for the surface contradictions persist, and it is only faith which enables man to accept the fact that underneath the meaninglessness there is meaning. Merton saw a special value in this rather hard-nosed but to him totally realistic view, for he felt it spoke directly to modern man, who, totally disillusioned by the crass inhumanity which has chiefly characterized the twentieth century, possessed of a profound distrust of the idea of the "innate goodness" of mankind, is completely closed to the glib, facile optimism which has so often marked popular religious attitudes. If modern man sees the world as absurd, he has to be told by the man of religion that he is right, but, further, that what he sees is not all there is. To accept the world as absurd, to accept the fact that there are many things in life which cannot be rationally explained or brushed aside with smiling assurances that everything is just fine, is not to deny God, but perhaps a necessary concomitant of the most important way of affirming him. It is not only the atheist who has to face nothingness, the void, but also, and especially, the believer, for the greatest kind of faith is that which does not abandon its longing for the light even when everything is surrounded by darkness. And this direct confrontation with the absurd, in faith not in despair, is deeply ingrained in the whole Christian tradition, as Merton liked to point out again and again. The favorite witness he brought to the stand in such instances was his beloved St. John of the Cross.

The emphasis upon Now, the supremacy and all-importance of the present moment, was another existentialist theme that Merton developed on various occasions. Too, he was taken by the existentialists' emphasis upon personalism. The idea of regarding the individual human person as of ultimate value, a concrete reality as opposed to merely a part of an abstraction such as "mankind" or "society," was, besides being a thoroughly Christian point of view, a necessary antidote to the depersonalizing and dehumanizing influences resulting from the spread of technology. But the individual was not a true person simply as a result of his individuality. For Merton, personhood was not an accident; it was a choice. In order to become a true person, which meant simply the person whom God wants one to be, one must, as we have seen, first become aware of and reject the false self with which one is burdened, an imposition of the depersonalized society in which one lives. This false self, which he often called the empirical self, is a mask which one wears, a role which one plays, to hide oneself from oneself. Once recognized for what it is, and repudiated, it ceases to become a hindrance to self knowledge. Rid of his false self, a man plumbs unencumbered to the depths of his being. There he discovers God, the Ground of his being. In discovering God he loses himself in him, and in losing himself in God he discovers his true self.

Anyone who reads Merton at all extensively is quickly made aware of the fact that he put a very high value on the concrete and a very low value on the abstract — evaluations which come out of the mainstream of existentialist thinking. For the most part, this attitude is clearly stated and convincing, especially when he integrates it with his advocacy of personalism. It is only when men cease to look upon other men as concrete human realities, and begin to look upon one another as abstractions—statistics, for example—that the way is paved for dehumanized action. Man's inhumanity to man, in other words, is the end result of reducing man to an abstraction. If an individual person—who lives and loves, who has joys and fears and who thrives on hope—is transformed into "jap," "kraut," "gook," "whitey" or "nigger," he is thereby rendered much easier to kill. He loses his personhood, his humanity, and becomes a symbol. Symbols are cheap, a dime a dozen.

But for all the poignant insights which emanated from Merton's attitude toward the concrete and abstract, here was a case in point where he often used jargon somewhat carelessly. He would, for example, Sometimes refer simply to "the concrete," in the abstract as it were, leaving the reader to wonder: The concrete what? More seriously, he allowed himself to hold too sour an opinion of abstraction, even when, by doing so, he got himself in positions which were logically unsound. The point is this: Merton, by too roundly condemning the process of abstraction, suggesting at times that it was the source of all man's ills, was simply refusing to acknowledge how inextricably human this process was. Would man be man if he could not make abstractions? Closer to home: Could he provide distinctions like that between "concrete" and "abstract" if he could not make abstractions? What is the concept which we identify as "concrete," after all, but simply another abstraction? In the end, therefore, it has to be recognized that Merton's dichotomy, in the manner in which he sometimes employed it, was a faulty one. It did not designate a clear distinction and hence was not doing the job he had staked out for it.

Perhaps it was the emphasis existentialism put on freedom, and, simultaneously, on human choice, which most attracted

Merton to this philosophy. At any rate, he put these ideas to very effective use in his own thought. One of the things that particularly disturbed him about much contemporary analysis of social problems, fostered by certain schools of psychology and sociology, was the tendency to eradicate personal guilt, hence personal responsibility. Though Merton was not incapable of subscribing to the idea of collective guilt—as his writings on racism show—he felt that no larger guilt ever eradicated the guilt which rests upon each and every individual. Collective, or participatory, guilt did not appear out of nowhere and insidiously impose itself on an otherwise innocent citizenry; it resulted from individuals who did evil acts and other individuals who implicitly condoned those acts by their silence. Because Merton passionately believed in the freedom of man, he just as passionately believed in his responsibility. And that freedom, that responsibility, are found—not as abstract ideas but as concrete realities—only within the individual. It is the individual, then, and the choices he makes that ultimately determine whether the world at large is going to be a better or a worse place in which to live. We can see that Merton believed this to be a fundamental truth throughout his life, even when, in the sixties, he was advocating legislative social reform. Such legislated reform, given the exigencies of modern society, was essential, but it would never work, it would never take hold, unless the individual person also chose to reform himself. Some, rather peremptorily it seems to me, have labeled this point of view crudely conservative and refused to take it seriously. Quickly slapping unapproving labels on ideas is a time-honored method of intellectual side-stepping; it is the easiest way of avoiding having to think about them. This particular idea—that society will be reformed only when individuals reform—though itself often used as an evasion, is in essence as sound as a rock. How could one really suppose that the case could be otherwise, unless, of course, one is no longer thinking about a society of free human beings but simply a collection of mindless robots, all properly programmed so as consistently to behave according to a big-brother's Master Plan.

In summary, it can be said that Merton was an existentialist, not to the degree that he was a philosophic thinker who carefully developed a system of thought, but rather to the degree that he incorporated into his wide and rambling world view—and once having incorporated them often embellished them imaginatively—many of the central tenets of the existentialist movement. He once said that being an existentialist means having certain experiences and attitudes rather than adhering to a given system of thought. I think that this description fits his case very well.

Like so many of the other interests which bloomed in his mature years, Merton's interest in oriental philosophy and religion can be traced back to his youth. One recalls, from *The Seven Storey Mountain*, his meeting and being deeply impressed by the Hindu monk Bramachari while a student at Columbia, a meeting which inspired him to dip into some of the oriental religious classics. It is interesting that Merton never completely lost touch with Bramachari. That his first permanent link with the East should have been a monk is significant, for we see that in later years, when his interest in and knowledge of the Orient began to expand, it was primarily by reason of the bridges he was attempting to build between western and eastern monasticism. For Merton personally, monasticism was the most important common denominator between East and West, as it was also between Christianity and the other major religions of the world. We note that it is principally that religion's monastic and/or mystical tradition which draws him, respectively, to Mohammedism, Judaism, Hinduism and Buddhism.

There have been some people, observing Merton's growing interest in oriental religions in the later years of his life, especially in Zen Buddhism, who have concluded that Merton's commitment to Christian teaching was beginning to weaken. About the only thing that such conclusions indicate is a decidedly superficial understanding of Merton and his thought on the part of those who arrive at them. What is most important to realize is that Merton, right from the outset, never looked upon Zen as a rival to Christian belief but, quite to the contrary, as something which could supplement and support it. One does not need to be overly erudite to be aware of the fact that to speak of oriental "religions" at all, in the sense in which we usually use the term, is to speak loosely. This is especially so when we speak of Zen, but also, at least in many of its manifestations, of Buddhism as well. Zen, as Merton pointed out, is like existentialism in that its devotees are not characterized by an adherence to a set of beliefs or a body of doctrine but rather by a way of experiencing life, a peculiar attitude toward reality. If we want to call Merton a Buddhist, then—and I certainly see no harm in doing so—it should be, as Father John Eudes Bamberger, OCSO, has suggested, in the same way that we would call him an Augustinian or Thomist, or, as I have called him, a Romantic. In other words, his being a Buddhist was in no wise contradictory to nor a diminishment of his being a Christian.

Many of the things which appealed to him in existentialism were precisely the things which appealed to him in the Zen Buddhist tradition, most of all the emphasis which that tradition put upon concrete reality rather than abstract concepts. The Zen man is most concerned with freeing himself from illusion and establishing permanent contact with reality, which is to say, atuning himself with the pulse of the universe, becoming one with ultimate truth. Just what illusion was as opposed to reality in any given instance Zen does not make clear, not because it is trying to be difficult but rather because it claims that it cannot be made clear, at least not through concepts and words. The way to reality is an experiential process rather than an intellectual one; after you have arrived you will know you are there, maybe. The problem is compounded by the fact that many who are convinced they have left illusion behind and discovered reality are in that very conviction suffering from illusion. Be that as it may— and the more one talks about Zen, by definition, the more obscure it becomes—Merton borrowed much from this Zen concern with illusion and employed it in many wide-ranging generalizations. One of his oft repeated observations was that western civilization as a whole was characterized by a commitment to an illusory rather than to a real reality, that illusory reality being materialism. The reverse side of this observation was that eastern civilization was virtually without flaw. This simplification, which he often fell into but which he was not totally unaware of, was no doubt caused by the intensity of his admiration and enthusiasm for eastern culture and its philosophical and religious traditions. Although his knowledge of those traditions was broad, and in some instances of impressive depth, it was not coupled with a comparable knowledge of oriental history, especially social history, and Merton did not become personally acquainted with the current realities of eastern civilization until the last few months of his life. My point is that his knowledge of the East was almost entirely theoretical in nature, and based upon a reading of that civilization's highest forms of literature. This being so, it is not surprising that the opinion he generally held of Eastern civilization was biased considerably in its favor.

Surely the most significant thing about Merton's pursuit of oriental studies was the ecumenical tone it often took. As was evidenced by his dialogue with the Japanese Zen scholar D. T. Suzuki, he was concerned with establishing bonds of affection and understanding between men of the East and the West who he felt already had something very important in common in their dedication to mysticism. But, on a larger plane than the strictly religious or philosophical one, he was also interested in breaking down the wall of mutual ignorance which for too long had separated eastern and western cultures generally. He said he was convinced that the West stood to learn something from the East, although he was not too sure—again displaying the bias alluded to above—that the East could learn anything worth while from the West.

There is reason to believe that he was seriously considering, through his studies, working toward a kind of philosophico-theological synthesis between East and West. I do not at all mean the kind of eclectic, watered-down mish-mash that one finds in, say, nineteenth century Transcendentalism where East did meet West, but in a way that did justice to neither. Merton explicitly revealed his distaste for such haphazard melanges because, no matter how well intentioned, they more often than not resulted in serious distortions of both traditions. Rather, it seemed Merton had in mind the kind of integration—oriental thought specifically Zen, into Christian theology—that St. Thomas Aquinas had effected by incorporating Aristotelian philosophy into the Christian tradition. This analogy is my own, and I do not mean to suggest by it that Merton conceived of himself as a potential twentieth century Angelic Doctor. I am sure he did not. The totally hypothetical question remains whether Merton, if his life had not been cut off when it was, could have effected such a synthesis. My inclination is to say that he would not have been able to do so, not for want of any interest or energy on his part, but simply because he was not the kind of thinker and systematizer which such a monumental project would demand. He would have continued to roam freely among the masterpieces of eastern culture and in his inimitably random way weave into his own thought those things which appealed to him and leave aside those things which did not. His was the curiosity of the prophet rather than that of the philosopher.

But the fact is that Merton, within the parameters of his own method, accomplished a great deal as it was. The writing he left on eastern philosophy and religion is remarkable for its breadth, its incisiveness, and for its clarity and eminent readibility. Although he was not immune from sometimes getting entangled in his own words, in general his explications of such complicated and exasperating matters as the principles of Zen stand as minor masterpieces of lucidity. Only someone who had dug deep and examined closely could have explained so well.

Merton never considered his study of the eastern cultural tradition as an idle avocation, but rather as an integral part of his calling as a monk. He felt that it was for the modern monk to engage himself in preserving what was best in all contemporary cultures, as was done by monks in the past, for all cultures, with their art and literature and philosophy and religion, are in one degree or another a reflection of the infinite goodness of God, an echo of his voice. He agreed enthusiastically with Pope Pius XII in his declaration that the Christian religion has no deathless commitment to any given culture but belongs to all cultures. And it was in the warmth of this conviction that he so solidly admired the sixteenth century Jesuits who, working in China, completely divested themselves of the accoutrements of western civilization and became totally assimilated into Chinese culture, without for a moment ceasing to be Christians and Jesuits. Merton immersed himself in Eastern lore not because he was seeking an alternative to Christianity but because he wanted to enrich a Christianity which, culturally speaking, he felt had in many ways gone stale. He was not looking for anything essentially new because he realized there was nothing essentially new to be found. The core of life's meaning he had already found, and that core, that Christ, he was sure lay as much at the depths of Buddhism as he lay at the depths of everything else. It was just a matter of digging, and in the process—this was the promise, this was the hope—opening up a way to that core-Christ who would be for millions of men, because of the circumstances of their life and culture, the most natural and meaningful.

A FUNNY KIND OF OPTIMISM

THOMAS MERTON WAS A PESSIMIST. One no-
tices, as a fairly consistent pattern throughout his life,
that the gloomier side of things tended to leave a greater
impression on him than the brighter side. He was more sensitive to how the world could go wrong than how it could go
right. This characteristic is explainable in great part, I suspect,
in terms of temperament. Most pessimists are so not by choice
but by reason of natural propensity; it's their bent. Just as
someone like Teilhard de Chardin was by nature an optimist,
in spite of all kinds of experiences seemingly very capable of
persuading him to be otherwise, so Merton, also often in the
face of telling evidence favoring the opposing view, was by
nature a pessimist.

But Merton's pessimism was by no means entirely of an
unconscious and involuntary kind. He himself was certainly
aware of the pessimistic strain in him. It is to be found implicitly throughout his writings, and at times, especially in
letters, he makes explicit reference to it. There was, indeed, a
certain purposefulness in Mertons's bringing his pessimism to
the forefront of his consciousness; it was to exploit it. The
chief result of his putting his pessimism to work, or, to state
it another way, the most dramatic manifestation of that pessimism, was his apocalyptic vision.

To Merton the apocalypse was the most appropriate meta-
phor for the twentieth century. He felt that many of the dire
eschatological happenings St. John described in the Book of

Revelations suggest much which is taking place in the present age. By establishing such a comparison he was, to be sure, indulging in a bit of poetic exaggeration, but not simply for the aesthetic satisfaction he may have derived from it. This was his way of dramatizing the seriousness of certain contemporary tendencies whose consequences for the human race as a whole he felt could be devastating, if not completely fatal. But, as he liked often to point out, when one is confronting such possibilities as global nuclear war, terms like "apocalyptic" and "end of the world" suddenly cease simply to be metaphors. They carry with them the disturbing potential of becoming very real realities. As a Christian Merton believed in the theological teachings concerning the end of history and the return of Christ, and although his pessimistic bent may have inclined him to suggest at times that the last days may in fact be upon the world, his considered opinion was always that, as the scriptures make clear, it is not for man to know matters which are locked in the inner secrecy of God's providential plan. Be that as it may, Merton seems to have thought there were certain positive practical results to be gained by acting *as if* the world were about to end. It was not a matter of indulging in mental masochism; much less was it by way of gleaning a self-righteous satisfaction in the conviction that all those wicked people "out there" were, like so many crumbs, going to be suddenly swept off the table of life and sent tumbling into the everlasting fires of hell. Rather, entertaining the serious possibility that one stands on the brink of disaster might encourage the critical first step (backward) in averting that disaster.

In a manner of speaking, the pessimist lives in very much a different world from those who do not share his way of looking at things. The pessimist and the non-pessimist may both be regarding the same realities, but the opinions they form of those realities are often substantially different. There is no question that Merton's pessimism notably affected his opinions on many matters. One recalls, for example, the bleak assessment of modern society, especially the urbanized, technological society of Western civilization, he was continually formulating. Understandably, a person would have to be completely insensitive not to recognize that that society is fraught with evil, but what also must be recognized, if any kind of realistic picture is going to be forthcoming, is that it also contains some good; and, in fact, that might be the more remarkable phenomenon. To recognize the water while gazing out to sea is no great accomplishment; to spot the white speck of sail flickering on the horizon, is. Merton, though he certainly was aware of the presence of good in the modern world, seldom talked about it; and that in itself is an important index of his pessimism.

A specific, and I think interesting, aspect of the pessimistic view he took of contemporary society in general was the manner in which he looked upon politicians. It was not complimentary. Merton found it difficult to consider people holding public office, whether elected or appointed, as worthy of anything approaching high esteem. To him they were by and large devious, self-serving individuals whose actions were founded infirmly on the sands of expediency and whose words carried about as much weight as a feather. While this attitude was a part of his pessimism, it must also be attributable to his idealism. No one is more sensitive than the idealist to the painful discrepancy between what is and what ought to be, and if he was hard on public officials it was also because he was acutely aware of the power and responsibility they had, the potential for doing good that power and responsibility lent them and, on the other hand, how little they were actually doing with that potential. In addition, by the umbrage he took toward politics and politicians, Merton was participating in a time-honored tradition in American culture. From at least the eighteenth century it has been customary in this country, especially among writers and intellectuals—one thinks, just offhand, of people like H. H. Brackenridge, Washington Irving, Mark Twain, H. L. Mencken and Norman Mailer—to take a rather supercilious attitude toward politicians, an attitude which often seemed to have been based upon a serious doubt as to the appropriateness of their being considered bona fide members of the human race. We recall that another group of people whom Merton looked askance at was contemporary American poets, because he felt that many if not most of them had prostituted their talents by not actively countering the demeaning influences of the political and cultural status quo. This peremptory judgment, not at all based on a careful appraisal of the situation, was also, I believe, a reflexive response of his pessimism. Often, in matters such as this, his somber mood caused him to project certain conclusions about a situation which the facts of that situation, once examined, would fail to corroborate.

The Church came under the cloud of Merton's pessimism in his later years, and so did monasticism. To be sure, he lost faith in neither institution, but in his writings of the sixties one can find a distinct lack of the ebullient (and indeed uncritical) enthusiasm for both which characterized his early years as a Catholic and a monk. Consistently, forms rather than essences were the cause of his chagrin. The Church always remained for him, in the innermost center of her being, the charismatic sign of Christ in the world. Regarded as such, she was without blemish and deserved unswerving, uncritical loyalty. But the total identity of the Church was not composed of this central, essentially divine, element; there was also the human element—the fallible flesh and blood men and women who filled out the contours of the Mystical Body of Christ on earth and whose duty it was to spread its spirit—and among this element there was much to find fault in and grow discouraged over. Merton was not always too specific about the kinds of things he saw wrong in the Church and which, he once remarked, a convert must blind himself to so as not to dampen his new-found faith. He did not, in other words, compose a list of grievances. By way of generalization, however, it can be said that what most disgruntled him about the Church was its tendency too readily to identify itself, by tacit acquiescence if by no other way, with political and economic power structures and their supporting ideologies. By so doing the Church was, by his estimate, succumbing to a worldly orientation, than which nothing could possibly be worse, for to him one of the primary functions of the Church was to stand markedly apart from the world, indeed, to stand in judgment upon it. While he obviously supported and encouraged radical reform within the Church, he did not sympathize—as his generally dim view of the Death of God movement shows—with those philosophies of reform which had made a shibboleth of "relevance" and which seemed driven by a frenetic passion to prove that Christianity was eminently capable of adjusting to the eccentricities of the modern world, even if the cost of such adjustment might be its becoming a pale and pathetic parody of what it once was. When Christians begin strainedly to insist upon their benevolent compatibility with the world, there is a good chance that they have already ceased to be Christians. To attempt to establish such an association is to become "of" the world, which would be to vitiate the Church's role within the unfolding drama of human history. There is a sense in which the committed Christian, by definition, must always be going against the mainstream of accepted opinion.

Reform in the Church was to be concentrated upon the effort to dissociate it from the power centers of either East or West, cleanse it of any complicity with forces which were identified by blantant disregard for human life and dignity and a cynical lack of concern for the true welfare of the race. At times he was encouraged, especially by encyclicals which had been published by Pope Pius XII and Pope John XXIII, by the belief that this kind of reform, albeit slowly, was in fact underway. Too, he took heart considerably at the convening of the Second Vatican Council; here, he felt, would be the main force behind turning the Church in the right direction, in awakening within it a healthy concern for the world in which it was immersed. But his pessimism, stirred up mainly, I am sure, by experiences which affected his personal life, acted as a brake on such encouragement. The fact that the American hierarchy, for one thing, was reluctant to speak out against what he regarded as the patent immorality of the Vietnam war, and, for another, was in some of its members the indirect cause of his being censored for his writings against that war, did nothing to lessen his conviction that an arbitrary, insensitive authoritarianism was too often the hallmark of too many Church leaders.

As was the case with the Church in general, his pessimism over monasticism had nothing to do with its essential nature. Certain structures had to be reformed, it went without saying. Specifically, many complicated and often cloying observances had to be excised from the monastic routine. The emphasis had to be removed from form and placed where it belonged, squarely upon spirit. In a word, the life had to be simplified. For Merton the key to monastic reform was to return to the straight-forward, ungnarled type of life envisioned by founders such as St. Benedict and followed by the early monks. But changing structures was far from everything and it is evident that he was not altogether happy with many of the alterations which had been brought about in his own monastery under the loudly flapping banner of renewal. A deep, well-educated respect for traditional monastic values prevented him from jumping on a band-wagon and succumbing to the silly conclusion that change equals improvement. While many changes were considered by him to be quite appropriate, others he thought to be shallow in conception and precipitous in implementation. He was pleased by the renovation of the monastic church, for one thing. Its heavy, cluttered atmosphere, the product of a combination of inept nineteenth century gothic revival architecture and an over-population of sentimental statuary, was replaced by one which is starkly yet serenely simple and very reminiscent of early Cistercian monastic churches. The decision to close up the monastic gift shop, and thus tone down a tendency to commercialize the monastery, was another step forward, in his opinion. When it came to liturgical reform, however, he could not get overly excited about many of the things which were going on. On a rational level, he felt that the switch from Latin to the vernacular was logically irrefutable, but emotionally he found it difficult to leave behind the limpid, unadorned beauty of the language which had sustained the liturgy with dignity and honor for centuries on end, especially when he heard some of the hurried, careless and aesthetically outrageous English translations which were replacing it. He reserved some of his more biting comments for those stabs at liturgical reform—and here he was referring to the Church at large—which appeared to be the results of a kind of aesthetic reductionism. There seemed to be a widespread conspiracy against beauty. The painful incompetence which seemed inevitably to crown these efforts was piously passed off by the perpetrators as a charismatic seal of approval: a virtue was made of doing something poorly so long as it was done in a spirit of pristine sincerity. Such demonstrations of folksy liturgical showmanship were supposedly intended to rekindle within the faltering faithful the bright flame of true devotion and undying Christian commitment. Merton was inclined to think that they would have just the opposite effect.

It might help, delving a little deeper into the nature of Merton's pessimism, to note that it displayed a fairly regular operational pattern, a pattern consisting of two stages. Putting it that way might sound rather forbidding, as if I were attempting to make a mechanistic analysis of a human being, but though my descriptive terms do have a certain stiffness about them I do not lose sight of the fact that they are being applied to a very pliant person. To state the case as simply as possible: Merton's pessimism observed and it generalized. In the first place, it heightened his consciousness and sharpened his focus. Because of his pessimistic tendency he was sharply aware of the flaws in life's fabric, of, to put it directly, the existence of evil. In this his pesimism served him well for an obvious reason, for one cannot begin to do anything about evil in the world until he recognizes its existence. So, for example, Merton observed, quite accurately, that there were politicians who were cunning, unscrupulous men and who, for that reason, were not to be trusted. But from acute observation Merton's pessimism led him to sweeping generalization, and in this it did not serve him well at all. He was too ready, on the basis of the recognition of specific evils, to conclude that those evils were either more pernicious or more pervasive than a dispassionate survey would have shown them to be. Thus to conclude, even by way of implication, that all politicians are corrupt from the discovery that some are corrupt is—besides poor logic—to assume a stance which does not reflect an altogether edifying responsibility. It was not that Merton was deliberately attempting to distort the picture, however. Pessimism by its very nature is emotional, and as such it has a tendency adversely to affect man's rational nature and contribute toward conceptions of reality which are consistently off-balance in their tiltings toward negativism.

This tendency to generalize about univeral evil on the basis of specific evil led Merton, as I think I have sufficiently demonstrated, to distort reality. At times these distortions were simply the result of his ignorance, the result in turn of his believing his generalization so thoroughly that he was not inspired to test its validity by checking it out against the facts. At other times, it must be recognized, Merton, fully aware that a given generalization was not verifiable in precisely the way it was stated, none the less employed it, not to deceive, but by way of bringing about a desired dramatic effect. Such conscious exaggeration can be a potent rhetorical device, and he used it with a great deal of skill. His pessimistic generalizations, however, be they conscious or unconscious, were not without their dangers, and occasionally they led him to take positions which were questionable at best and, at worst, well-nigh indefensible. Perhaps what I have already said has provided enough examples of this, but in order to clarify my point I would like to call attention to a specific issue. Merton's pessimism as directed against monasticism did not prove to be debilitating in his assessment of that institution, at least as far as it concerned him personally. When it came to considering monasticism as applied to others, however, this was not always the case, and in at least one instance he remarked that, given the present state of monasticism, he would be very reluctant to encourage anyone to enter the monastic life.

On the face of it this might appear to be an innocuous enough statement, but if we examine it closely, and if we consider its source it quickly assumes a tone which is not a little disconcerting. This is the only place of which I am aware in the entire corpus of Merton's published and unpublished writings where he gives even the slightest hint that he was not totally in accord with the Christian concept of vocation, that concept which holds that a monk, as well as every other person who follows the will of God, is what he is by reason of his choosing for himself what God has already chosen for him. A religious vocation, then, the vocation of a monk, is primarily a matter of responding to what is considered a special grace of God. One is perfectly free not to respond to such a grace, but doing so would be a rather risky business. As a matter of fact, there is no good reason to believe that Merton ever rejected this concept, but this only makes his statement all the more problematic. If a monastic vocation is primarily a matter of divine inspiration, one would suppose that the grace that engendered it would, if cooperated with, preserve it, no matter what admittedly difficult situations the individual would be subjected to in his efforts to be loyal to his calling. For someone who is disgruntled over certain of the structures of contemporary monasticism to discourage a person with a potential vocation from embarking upon the monastic life would be, it seems to me, a very presumptuous move.

But there is no doubt in my mind that Merton was not intending to be presumptuous. Again, it was his pesky pessimism which ended him up in binds like this, and it is a safe bet that, had the contradictoriness of his position been pointed out to him, he would have quickly taken pains to set the record straight. Indeed, the mainstream of his writings and thinking emphatically demonstrates that these kinds of erratic rivulets are not to be taken as characteristic of his general view. None the less, they are there, and they have to be recognized as genuine problems in his thought, an unfortunate effect of his pessimism.

We cannot contend with the fact of Merton's pessimism without seriously considering the possibility that, besides serving as a convenient explanatory factor for some of his

more jagged speculations, to some people it might be a
legitimate cause for scandal. We can imagine their reasoning
as going something like this: How is it that this man Merton,
a Christian and a monk, could entertain such a bleak outlook
on the world and reality? Is not a Christian supposedly a
man of faith, and does not his faith tell him that, no matter
how bad present circumstances may be, a Divine Providence
is ordering all things toward a delightful denouement? Is it
not the Christian's duty, then, mindful of this, to cast his
thoughts and words in an essentially positive mold? Should
not his voice, amid the stridently shouted prophecies of
doom which rankle our ears from every corner, should not
his voice be one of sure and soothing hope? Finally, and
particularly, was not Merton, through his pessimism, in effect
demonstrating the weakness of his faith, if indeed at times
not the lack of it?

The effort seriously to confront such a response to
Merton's pessimism can prove to be a very instructive exercise, for it can spur us to examine the phenomenon with the
utmost thoroughness, to get right to the bottom of it. Once
we have done so we are most apt to re-emerge from our
investigation with the conviction that those who are scandalized by Merton's pessimism thereby tell us more about themselves, and their rather superficial view of the Christian commitment, than they do about Thomas Merton and his world
view. It is not at all that they are wrong about his being
pessimistic, or that his pessimism had real pitfalls to it, but
to the degree to which they see that pessimism to be completely lacking in redeeming qualities they have stopped
short. They refrain from puncturing its surface, from dipping
deep within it and finding out what a potent positive force it
was in his life and thought. That Merton's pessimism should
have been at bottom a positive force—here is another of the
many paradoxes which marked his life.

In its general effects upon those who were exposed to his
writing, Merton's pessimism was a decidedly therapeutic
influence. It came as a quick, clean wind, scattering an especially opaque and noxious fog which had settled ominously

upon the landscape. Since the end of World War Two and the beginning of the Atomic Age, many Americans, perhaps more out of unconscious fear than malicious intent, had managed to adjust to the horrors of their age by the simple expedient of ignoring them. The 1950s were especially characterized by this escapist mentality. During this decade it was considered proper to tend one's own garden (or fallout shelter, as the case may be) and let the rest of the world fend for itself. It was a time when much was made of the need to be optimistic, to look on the brighter side, to think positively. But there was an unmistakable tinny tone to the optimism then being advocated. It was simply a corroboration of the general escapist mentality, for it was a blind optimism, an optimism which was urging people to flee facts, or paint over them prettily, rather than face up to them squarely. It was, in sum, nothing but an evasive tactic. The falsity, not to say danger, of this bogus optimism was dramatically and painfully brought to the fore when the fifties gave way to the sixties and the majority of Americans were made painfully aware that the society, which they had led themselves to believe was virtually without flaw in anything concerning essentials, proved to contain more than its share of flaws, and serious ones too. So many of the things which according to the head-hiding credo "could never happen here"—student revolts, urban riots, large scale resistance to the draft, a rash of political assassinations—were happening here with a vengeance. Yet for all the traumas of this rude awakening, there were still some who preferred to roll over and go back to sleep. There were the hippies, for example, as well as all those they influenced, who proclaimed a curse upon the house, opted for a kind of ignorance-is-bliss point of view, and lapsed into a benign, often narcotized, indifference. But there were also not a few churchmen who, proclaiming all opposition to a preconceived but eternally nebulous notion of the "American way of life" to be *per se* ungodly, called for a revivification of something very much like the easy optimism which was the trademark of the fifties.

It was against this fatalistic indifferentism to very real and very serious evils in American society, whether of the hippie who wanted to "tune out" from those evils or of the church- man who wanted to consider them as imagery, that Merton's pessimism stood, and indeed continues to stand, as a healthy antidote. He had very little patience with the idea that to be a Christian meant to be an optimist and to be an optimist meant to have a view of the world which was blind to the evil of which it was full, or short of that, to believe that despite all the evil everything was going to turn out okay, somehow. To him this was both a perversion of what it meant to be a Christian as well as a corruption of the best meaning of optimism. A Christian's optimism consisted, firstly, in frank- ly and fully admitting the existence of evil, and then, the critical factor, his actively attempting to eradicate that evil. It was only when all his energies were employed in the eradica- tion of evil that he could legitimately hope that evil was doomed to defeat because of, and only because of, powers far superior to his or to any other man's or to those of the human race taken all together. Merton's pessimism was a way of waking people up, of warning them against the dangers of being lulled into a sense of false security by fostering an "optimism" which was in reality an evasion of one's respon- sibilities, as a human being, to the family of man.

Earlier in this discussion I had occasion to draw a distinc- tion between the conscious and unconscious aspects of Merton's pessimism. It is by concentrating on its conscious aspects, the manner in which Merton deliberately fostered a pessimistic point of view, that we can see to what extent this was a positive force in his life.

In the first place, pessimism was always a means for him, never an end. He made use of this natural propensity to draw attention to things, his own attention as well as that of oth- ers. As such there was always a functional quality about it. We also observe that, for pretty much the same reason, it was tentative; a permanent pessimism was never part of the plan. This was not something he was advocating, holding up as an ideal to be sought after and imitated. A pessimistic view of the world was an expediency, and not altogether a pleasant one at that. It was after all not exactly a heart warming practice to keep oneself continually apprised of the gloomier aspects of life; and if those aspects did not exist, along with the obligation to do something about them, there would be no excuse at all for being a pessimist. If in fact we lived in a perfect world, pessimism would be a luxury, a characteristic which one would be inclined to associate with eccentrics, or masochists. But in a world such as ours it would seem that not to be a pessimist is to be an eccentric, and perhaps it might even be argued that not to be a pessimist is to be a masochist, for certainly one who does not have a properly dire attitude toward the modern world and its prospects is very likely submitting his psyche to a peculiarly subtle kind of punishment. Pessimism was not a game with Merton. It was not a means by which he derived any kind of neurotic satisfaction. Furthermore, though he did have a tendency to exaggerate on its account, it was never a cause of his inventing anything. Through it he saw the world's evils more keenly, felt them more acutely, but it called forth no visions out of vacuums. What he grew pessimistic about, anyone could have grown pessimistic about; it was just a matter of opening one's eyes to see what he saw.

Secondly, it is most important, when talking about this subject, to distinguish between pessimism and despair. To despair, in theological terms, is to abandon all hope of God's salvific influence taking effect upon you as an individual person or upon the world as a whole. It is to throw in the sponge, to quit, to sit down and wait for death to intone the anticlimatic end. It is to sin, in perhaps the most serious way possible. In discussing the theological virtue of hope, Merton had a habit of emphasizing that it was not to be equated with the superficial optimism which we have discussed above. Indeed, there is nothing at all incompatible in the fact of a person who is thoroughly imbued with the virtue of hope also being a pessimist, for his pessimism is directed toward the temporal imperfections of a fallen creation but his hope is lodged firmly in the eternal reality of God's providential solicitude for that creation. His pessimism does not cancel out his hope but in a sense reaffirms it; it is as it were an existential testament to that hope. It is a means by which a man explicitly declares to the world that he be committed to something infinitely more profound than what that world can offer him.

In this connection it is worthwhile to point out that Merton did allow for the appropriateness of what might be called a metaphorical despair. For example, he felt that it was not only proper but in fact the duty of the monk to "despair" of the world and its ways. To "despair" of the ugliness, the madness, the sheer and utter chaos of contemporary society is in effect to take the first step toward making an important act of faith. To "despair" of the pseudo-solutions which modern man puts forth for the problems which beset him is to put oneself in a good position for finding the true solutions to those problems. In a word, to "despair" of anything less than God was the monk's way of declaring his complete and unqualified hope in God alone.

The recognition that Merton's pessimism was not a negatively oriented, self-defeating fact of his life, is, finally, by way of admitting that it might be considered, as he himself considered it, a funny kind of optimism. There are certain people who demonstrate their deep affection for others, especially those for whom they feel responsible, by dealing with them harshly. In cases such as this the harshness must be interpreted; it is not to be taken at face value, for far from being a sign of animosity it is a sign of love. I think all of us are familiar with this paradoxical kind of human behavior, and rather than condemn it we more often than not admire it. For reasons which are not at all clear, there seems to be an added degree of genuineness to that affection which demonstrates itself covertly or by indirection; perhaps, so convinced are we of the possibilities of deception in such matters, we prefer the person who protests not enough to him who protests too much. However that might be, I think there are parallels here with respect to Merton's pessimism. We should not take it at face value. It was the protective disguise for an optimism which—who knows? —would probably have been too much for the cynical twentieth century to handle.

Before closing this discussion on his pessimism, I would like to conjecture that that which contributed significantly to keeping this natural inclination under the right kind of control and preventing it from becoming a detrimental influence in his life was his sprightly and irrepressible sense of humor. It has been observed that the real test of a true sense of humor is that the possessor can laugh at himself as readily as at anything else. Merton's sense of humor passed this test with flying colors. The ability to laugh at oneself implies a sense of perspective; a person is able to step back and form a balanced view of himself and his world. Merton, through his sense of humor, was constantly doing this. As a result, he was constantly evaluating his pessimism, among other things, against a background of larger realities. It therefore never got away from him, never became something which was controlling him rather than he it. When he got too serious he laughed at his own seriousness, thereby proving how truly and healthily a serious man he was; for a serious view is a clear view, and nothing is a better assurance against its blurring than laughter. When he got too pessimistic he laughed at his own pessimism, putting it in its proper context, and revealing the vigorous brand of optimism, the hope which lay at the bottom of his being.

A MODEL

THERE IS MORE THAN ONE WAY of being a middle-of-the-roader. The worst way is by avoiding decisions, the best way is by making them. Some people are in the middle of the road simply because they consider it safer there. Their position is explained in terms not of their having carefully considered both sides of a question but rather of their having made a concerted effort to ignore the question altogether. Their position can be interpreted as a demonstration of moral cowardice. But there are other people for whom being in the middle of the road is the result of a deliberate, reasoned decision on their part. Having scrutinized both sides of a question they see it as folly to opt for one side to the total exclusion of the other, for in effect each side represents an unacceptable extreme. The only logical conclusion they can make is to reject both in some respects and accept both in some respects, thereby putting themselves in the middle. In assuming this stance, they are fully aware of the precariousness of their position. It lacks the security which comes from being snugly ensconced in one or another of the "infallible" positions on either side of the road. Then too, being in the middle by choice rather than by default, continuing to communicate with both sides to guard against becoming rigid in one's professed flexibility, is very often to call down upon oneself the plagues of both houses. Few things are more onerous to extremists than to be confronted with people who habitually refuse to look at life simplistically, who decide to steer between the treacherous shallows and the turbulent deeps. For all that, however, those who so decide are not left without a certain reassuring conviction of the basic soundness of their way.

Thomas Merton, in his life and in his thought, kept consistently to the middle of the road, and he did so by reason of deliberate choice. The *via media* was his way, in other words, and, given the circumstances of his times, this was probably his strongest characteristic. It certainly was his most edifying.

Merton came into his own as a thinker, matured as a human being, during a time when the cultural fabric of Western civilization, which had been placed under severe strain almost from the very beginning of the twentieth century and which over the course of that century had suffered some serious rents, was seemingly in danger of being torn to shreds. Since the ominous ending of World War Two western man has been in a dither of questioning and self-doubt. The large and comfortable cultural edifice which had been built up over the centuries, which was founded on a general consensus concerning what were taken to be immutable truths, and which had lent to his ancestors a vivifying sense of identity and purpose, seemed suddenly on the verge of collapsing. That foundation of immutable truths was crumbling beneath him. All sense of smug comfort, all sense of being at home if not in the universe at least within what was considered a superior and eminently righteous way of life, was gone in a puff. In place of purpose, confusion came. To be a western man meant to be disoriented in more ways than one. One scarcely believed in one's identity unless it was shaken and shaped by crisis.

The reactions to this situation were predictably various. It appeared that the majority—as is perhaps always true of the majority in all places and all times—simply did not recognize the problem as a problem. They made no response. Whether this was the result of ignorance or choice, or a combination of the two, will have to be left for the intellectual historians and social psychologists to figure out. Then there were some people who, having had the problem pointed out to them, being apprised of the cracks in the foundation and the tilt of the building, chose to reject the evidence of their eyes. They protested that there was nothing at all the matter with western civilization and that anyone who would argue otherwise was an unprincipaled and cynical defeatist, as well as, more likely than not, a Communist. Next, there were those who, while seeing and acknowledging the reality of the serious defects in the cultural edifice, were not prepared to admit that these need necessarily be catastrophic. The edifice could yet be saved, and they called for workers to begin the arduous process of repair. A fourth reaction to this situation was displayed by a group whose members seemed to derive pleasure from the thought that the collapse of western civilization was at hand. In fact they sometimes expressed a willingness to help the process along. Let the whole thing come crashing down, they argued, for it is rotten through and through. Once it is demolished we can clear away the rubble and start anew.

I speak of this crisis in the past tense, but of course there is nothing past about it at all. It is very much with us. My purpose in dealing with it primarily as history is to consider it in terms of Merton's association with it. This pervasive consciousness that things were falling apart probably hit its peak in this country during the 1960s and was inextricably entertwined with the domestic crisis over the Vietnam War. Merton, as we have seen, first, had since his youth been possessed with the conviction that there was something drastically wrong with Western civilization, and second, was adamantly opposed to the Vietnam war. In fact he was among the first of the American intellectuals to raise his voice against it. What supposedly we had, then, was the perfect overlapping of a personal view and a pervasive one. Well, not quite, for while Merton no doubt felt a certain amount of gratification in the fact that many Americans were beginning seriously to question what hitherto they had reckoned as beyond questioning, that is, to see the moral corruption rampant in contemporary society, he did not sympathize with either the self-righteous complacency or the deranged panic which often accompanied this new apprehension of reality. He observed that certain Americans, intellectuals especially, had a way of roundly condemning the sickness of the American way of life and then, their duty done, washing their hands of it so they could without distraction draw into their little walled-in worlds and "do their thing," not without, however, continuing to take every advantage of the material benefits which that utterly disgusting way of life provided. Perhaps because he himself was constantly tempted just to let the world go, let it boil in its own poisonous stew, he was particularly sensitive to the indefensibleness of this reaction. Such Romantic rugged individualism, if it ever did have a legitimate currency, was in the present circumstances definitely obsolete. And as for those who slapped the culture with one hand and got all they could from it with the other, this was simply a variation on a classic syndrome—wanting to condemn one's cake and eat it too.

One the other hand, neither could he go along with those for whom the new, darker vision of America sent into a tailspin of despair. Commonly, the most reliable index of this despair was a frenzy of mindless activity. Merton was all for action. He believed that the problems in the world were solvable—or, to put it in a way he often did, evil was not irreversible— and that consequently men of conscience and good will were obligated to work toward the solution of those problems. But he also made a distinction between action and activism. Action was activity with a purpose. Activism was purposeless activity; it was activity for the sake of activity. He saw through the altruistic disguise in which activism often clothed itself. He listened to its loud protests of good will, noted the peculiar stridency in the tone, and concluded that it protested too much. He saw that activism, rather than being motivated by hope, was in fact an expression of despair. Activism was a form of *divertissement*, a means of distracting these engaged in it from their own deep convictions that all was lost, that what they were doing was, apart from its distracting qualities, meaningless and futile.

There was therefore a certain conscious pointlessness to the activity itself. It was a way of confronting an absurd situation by what might be called tactics of counter-absurdity. Protests were not so much against something as against everything. The activist, in his despair, transformed what was declaredly a gesture of concern for others into a means of punishing them for daring to have the affrontery of not sharing wholeheartely in his own despair. Merton repudiated this reaction because he failed to see how, in its essence, it was in any way different from the position of the complacent intellectual. It was, in the end, a luxury, a bit of masochistic self-indulgence which the world could ill afford.

In a less general matter, in the situation which prevailed in the Catholic Church in the aftermath of the Second Vatican Council, we see another good example of how Merton kept his head about him and became a spokesman for the sanity of the *via media*. One of the sadder consequences of the Council was a strict pairing off between two perhaps equally vociferous factions within the Church, conservative and progressive—to use the names most usually attached to them. This division, though it seemed to come about overnight and from nowhere, was in truth but the long-delayed rising to the surface of something which had existed in latent form within the Church for many years. It is probably safe to surmise that the majority of Catholics can be put in neither of these two camps, maybe because they have the simple good sense to see that there is a boisterous posturing in both, and that neither—their adamant protestations to the contrary—have exclusive possession of the Keys of the Kingdom. Conservatives and progressives alike, with that steely-eyed conviction of being right and nothing but right which seems to be the chief mark of the over-anxiously religious, have been railing at us and one another ever since the Council closed. The end result of their various positions and proclamations has been the production of an atmosphere heavy with dissension and distrust. They seem dedicated to a divisiveness which too often appears simply gratuitous, and yet they both insist that unity is their guiding principle. Both groups seem totally incapable of the kind of magnanimity, of healthy self-doubt, which Benjamin Franklin urged upon the delegates at the Constitutional Convention so that they would not indulge in petty bickering and accomplish something besides making noise. They seem more concerned with solidifying their own vaguely defined positions and scoring points against the pitiful opponent than with working toward the creation of a milieu which could truly be called Catholic.

Although Merton in many cases agreed with positions taken by progressives, he stopped far short of identifying completely with them. It has already been observed that toward the matter of flamboyant liturgical reform, a progressive sacred cow, he was considerably less than respectful. And while he had his own bones to pick when it came to a discussion of authority in the Church, he would not condone the kind of puerile flaunting of legitimate authority often engaged in by progressives. For Merton, authority and freedom were not mutually exclusive but rather dependent upon one another. When the power of those in authority was balanced by the freedom of the governed, then a healthy situation obtained. But should one over balance the other, as he felt often was the case when the exercise of authority became excessive or somewhat less than prudent, then measures had to be taken to correct the situation. But he found it silly to suppose that one is making a convincing case for the recognition of one's maturity as a human being by acting in a manner which is unconscionably immature. The child who jumps up and down and screams because he feels adults are failing to treat him as a "big boy" is thereby only underscoring the extent to which he is in fact a child, while at the same time solidifying the adults in the very attitude he is protesting.

He saw something to sympathize with in the conservatives' deference for tradition, but if his attitude were studied closely it would be shown to be considerably different from theirs. Merton's love for tradition was not blind and indiscriminating. Just as he made no facile equation between change and improvement, so also he did not think that because something was of the past it was *ipso facto* to be preferred. The past, like the present, contained both its good and bad. His idea of a healthy respect for the past was to pick out and preserve only the good which it has brought to us. The truly good is timeless. Those conservatives who tenaciously clung to the nonessentials of the past—oftentimes of the fairly recent past—and attempted to make essentials of them were in effect attesting to a form of superstition. When they attached almost absolute value to the Latin language while seemingly ignoring what the Latin (or the vernacular, for that matter) was saying, they did little to bolster their credibility. It is not a sin to harbor a warmly nostalgic regard for the past, and who would want too quickly to condemn those who genuinely lament the supplanting of much which they considered beautiful and symbolically alive. But it is quite a different thing to place oneself in bull-headed opposition to change either because of a childish unwillingness to surrender ways whose effects are more therapeutic than truly religious or because of a cranky conviction that the perpetrators of change are insane, if not downright diabolical.

In happy contrast to the vitriolic, decidedly uncharitable manner in which conservatives and progressives have demonstrated themselves capable of dealing with one another, Merton's tone was prevalently temperate. It is true that he was quite skilled at stating his views in no uncertain terms, but never do you find him launching the scathing *ad hominem* attack which is the desperate recourse of little men. It was wrong ideas that got him angry more than wrong people, and he never forgot how to make the separation between the idea and the person who holds it. Just as the theologian condemns the sin and not the sinner, so the intellectual should condemn the thought and not the thinker. In a word, Merton was motivated first and last by the law of love. If a man is avowedly struggling for the triumph of the truth, it is imperative that he realize that truth and love are inseparable. You do not serve the truth by speaking of and to your neighbor who does not agree with you in words which are calculated to kill. In Merton we see a man who still believed you could catch more flies with a teaspoon of honey than with a barrel full of vinegar, who, on a much deeper level, believed that love was the *sine qua non* foundation upon which any hoped-for unity within the Church or within the world at large was going to rest. For all his passion for ideas, he was a man who attached more importance to winning a friend than winning an argument. Here again, his preference for the concrete person over the abstract idea.

It has been said more than once already that Merton was not a systematic thinker, that, as a result, his writings do not compose a strongly coherent, highly organized unity. But this is not to say that all is helter-skelter, that there are not certain unifying elements which, for all its diversity, do not draw his thought into a detectable, albeit loose, whole. It was primarily the eclectic quality of his mind and interests which explained this diversity; the unity, on the other hand, was in great part attributable to his love for balance, his reluctance to go off in any one direction to the extent that he completely lost sight of the possibility that there might be other directions as well. Merton was a maker of distinctions. For all his occasional impatience with (not to mention indulgence in) simplistic thinking, he more often than not refused to fight fire with fire. If someone is calling gray, white, you accomplish nothing whatever by retorting that it is black. Rather, you must grapple with the complexity of its grayness. He loved to examine a thought, an issue, from several possible sides, especially in his meditative writing, and he recognized the wisdom in admitting that at times the most appropriate thing he could say about an issue was that he could not say anything about it. The reverse side of this love of analysis, of making distinctions, was his conviction that there are certain matters that defy exhaustive analysis and for which distinctions have as much applicability as water to the proverbial duck's back. Put another way, he had the profoundest of respect for paradox. His interest in and almost at times devotion to paradox was a manifestation of his more pervasive interest in mystery. Paradox is a kind of mystery. For him mystery was not something confined to the realms of religion or theology. Mystery was the poetry of life, and every aspect of life, even the most prosaic, was shot through with it. Mystery illuminated life, but its light was blinding. It was best then simply to accept it for what it was and one's limitations for what they were. Rejoice in its light and bask in its warmth.

Ralph Waldo Emerson once made the comment, by way of emphasizing the importance of the influence of Goethe on nineteenth century writers that, "Goethe was the cow from which all the milk was drawn." The literary historian and critic F. O. Matthiessen felt that although Emerson did not produce a single work worthy of being called a masterpiece, his writings taken as a whole, the ideas he developed in them, greatly influenced his contemporaries and have had a profound effect on the subsequent development of American culture. This, besides being a sound assessment of Emerson and his influence, comes very close, in my opinion, to the kinds of generalizations which could be made about Merton apropos of any discussion of the influence of his thought. At least it can provide a productive point of departure.

Merton was comparable to Emerson in more than one respect. Perhaps the most important trait he shared with him was the fact of his being an essentially religious thinker. Both men were dedicated anti-materialists; both believed that the Real Reality lay beyond the surface realities, and that man only came into his own as a man when he realized that his deepest identity was spiritual. Merton reflected Emerson's penchant for solitude as well as his general discomfort with the crassness of American commercialism. He could match his love of nature with Emerson's and also his innate antipathy toward war and militarism. As to the latter, one is reminded of Emerson's remark: "I do not like to see a sword at a man's side. If it threaten man, it threatens me. A company of soldiers is an offensive spectacle." Of special significance is the fact that Merton, like Emerson, was an eclectic thinker. He ranged far and wide to collect the material which he wove into his works, visiting many centuries and many cultures. His mind regarded all borders as artificial, the feeble fabrications of the academic mind. A case might be made for the contention that the most natural art form for the eclectic thinker is the essay. At any rate, this was the form in which Merton excelled, and of course the essay was also Emerson's main vehicle of communication and artistic expression.

In terms of what has been said in previous chapters, I hope that a reasonsably convincing brief has been presented for the argument that Merton, through his life and writings, exerted a substantial influence on his contempories. As any intellectual historian is aware, it is difficult if not impossible to come up with airtight empirical evidence to demonstrate the amount of influence a given figure and the ideas he propounded may have had on the people who lived and the events which happened during his era. In the realm of social science, the lines between cause and effect are none too clear. This much being admitted, however, it has also to be recognized that there is a considerable amount of space this side of absolute certitude in which one can legitimately move around. After careful observation and sober reflection, one is allowed, taking care to strike the proper tone of tentativeness, to broach as worthy of serious consideration matters for which one has not accumulated a stunning array of statistics. When we talk about Merton's importance as measured by his influence, there are certain generalizations which I would not hesitate to make. The first is that he, by reason of his dynamic concern for social issues, specifically the questions of war and race, is to be regarded as among the leaders of those American intellectuals who, primarily during the sixties, brought about a large scale resurgence of social consciousness. If we view Merton exclusively from within the context of religion, his stature and influence increase. He was widely translated, and on the international level his reputation could be considered comparable to that of a Karl Barth and a Martin Buber. Domestically, he was one of the major religious figures of the twentieth century. His name will loom large in any subsequent history of religion in America.

What will be the nature and extent of Merton's influence in the future is, of course, hard to say. We are still too close to him to be able adequately to determine whether his works will have a lasting quality. My hunch, though, is that his influence will increase rather than diminish over the years. *The Seven Storey Mountain* was a very popular book when it was published in 1948, but the fact that it continues to sell on a steady basis indicates that its popularity was no passing fad. Apart from the natural interest and inspiration it will continue to provide for Catholics, it will also last, in my estimate, as one of the exemplars of the autobiographical genre within American literature, and I would not be altogether surprised to see it turn into a classic in that respect. The stylistic simplicity and irreproachable sincerity of books like *Seeds of Contemplation* will very likely insure that they too will be preserved as a significant addition to our literature. Finally, I think that there is a permanent place for his journals, for, besides the fact that they contain some of his best writing, they provide much rich material for establishing relationships which link the man, his views, and the world in which he lived.

But I do not think that Merton's literary survival is going to depend so much on the force and durability of given works as it will on the total impact of his life and thought, and in this the comparison with Emerson is most fruitful. If it is true that many of his ideas were either poorly developed or not developed at all it was not because those ideas were not viable, that they did not contain a great deal of potency. It was simply not his gift to develop, to systematize. But it was very much his gift to discover, not new ideas necessarily, but new, imaginative and promising relationships between ideas. He was essentially an explorer of the mind; he roamed new seas and opened up new territories. It will be up to others to pick up where he left off, to move into those territories and settle down, and once settled down thoroughly to map out the terrain. Merton, as was true of Emerson and Goethe before him—although not to the same degree as either—will become a rich source from which many will draw the milk of inspiration. The seminal nature of his thought as applied to such matters as the relationship between the individual and the community and the universal aspects of monasticism, those aspects which transcend cultural and religious differences—to name only two of many areas—will provide much valuable raw material with which students and disciples can work for years to come. It will be for these followers of Merton to develop fully the various implications of his thought, to bring to full term the many ideas which he left in an embryonic state. I sometimes have the feeling—though not at all to diminish the remarkable quality of his own achievement—that Merton might come to be known in intellectual history primarily for what he inspired in others.

Intellectual history aside, there were other exceptional qualities in Merton, ethical qualities, which dramatically set him apart from the ordinary run of men and which, along with the intellectual qualities, establish him as a model for our age and ages to come. Merton was a man of perseverance. Offhand, this might appear to be a quality of dubious worth and perhaps some would consider it stretching a point to proclaim it as a virtue. Qualifications are in order. In the first place, perseverance is not obstinancy. To stick to something because you are obsessed by a mindless fear of being called a quitter, or because you do not want to admit you were wrong in your initial decision, or because you are eccentric and derive a perverted enjoyment from being tenacious simply for the sake of being tenacious, do not constitute commendable attitudes. A man who continues along a freeway at seventy miles an hour after he realizes he has taken the wrong turnoff at the last interchange and is consequently on the wrong road is not a man of perseverance; he is crazy. Quite obviously, these are not the kinds of things I have in mind in calling attention to Merton's perseverance. A man of perseverance is one who stays to the end with things which, by their very nature, are worthy of his terminal dedication. He is a man for whom language has not become corrupt, who still sees a connection between words and reality. Because he rejects the idea that men live in an absurd universe, he rejects as well the concomitant notion that language is a vehicle of absurdity. For him words still count, they still mean. He is a man of his word, which is to say that when he gives it the recipient can rest assured that the spirit in which it was given is not dying a slow but inevitable death in the heart of the giver. Making a commitment for the man of perseverance is a public declaration that, come what may, he will see things through. He will not stop until he has done the task he has promised to do, and there is nothing perfunctory or half-hearted in the manner in which he goes about it. Perseverance is a type of courage, for it implies that you do not give up when the going gets rough. It implies the understanding that if something had intrinsic value in the beginning, it will have it in the middle and it will have it at the end. To make a long-term commitment is obviously a risky business, if for no other reason because human beings lack the ability to read the future. Sometimes, on account of the fact that no storms intervene between the making and the fulfillment of it, a commitment presents no problems. More often than not, however, circumstances arise—personal crises, external pressures, the lassitude that naturally follows upon long passages of time—which make the fulfillment of a commitment a severe test of moral fiber. When it became evident that a commitment was going to cost them something, lesser men have always been able to find reasons for quickly and conveniently abandoning it. A common tactic is to contend that in making the commitment they either did not know what they were doing, or were intending by it something other than what most men would intend by it. On the other hand, the greats of history have been consistently characterized by their ability to stand by that to which they have dedicated and committed themselves, and this in the face of the most trying of difficulties, sometimes, indeed, in the face of death.

It would be pathetic to make a virtue of perseverance understood only as obstinancy, but it would be no less pathetic, as our age in effect seems to have done, to make a virtue of the total lack of perseverance, rightly understood. We live in a time when a very low premium is put upon the desire or ability to dedicate oneself to the long-term and the difficult. Our exemplars are too often those who are dedicated to purposelessness, people whose energies are expended in a dizzying round of breaking off and starting anew in the vain hope that in one of their desperately contrived encounters they are going to find themselves. The fact that we talk so much about commitment is the best indication that it is virtually non-existent among us, as is also true of something else we discuss a great deal, communication. We have visited terrible abuses upon language, to the extent that one sometimes wonders if the damage done is not irreparable. Words no longer seem to take hold with us. They have become noises. We seem more and more incapable of believing one another, at times we scarcely believe ourselves. Loyalty is the most ephemeral of realities. What we normally mean when we say a man is loyal is that he is linked to a position in which he is having as many of his selfish desires filled as possible; if he were to find in a second position greater opportunities for such fulfillment his loyalty to the first would disappear in a wink.

Merton stood out in a dramatic contrast against this dreary background of moral tepidity and vacillation. He demonstrated the quality of his perseverance in many readily apparent ways, in his lasting commitment to his faith, to his priesthood, to the monastic order to which he belonged, and to his friends and counselees. At the bottom of all his various loyalties, and lending them all strength and direction, was an abiding loyalty to his own best self. Merton knew himself very well, and whereas that knowledge apprised him of his foibles and weaknesses it also made him aware of his strengths, and he had faith in these strengths. Because he had faith in himself he could have faith in others, and because he had faith in others he could have faith in institutions. It worked that way because there was no other way in which it could have worked.

If Merton had an expansive mind, he had a heart to match it. Truly, he was a person of almost limitless expansiveness. I think adequate discussion has been given to the fact that he was always receptive to new ideas, always straining to push back the frontiers of ignorance or inadequacy and extend his intellectual horizons. He brought the same kind of attitude to his personal relationships with other people. Merton embraced the world. His untrammeled openness to others, the disarming genuineness and sincerity with which he dealt with all with whom he came in contact, was posited upon a deep respect for their persons and (in most cases at least) an unprejudiced regard for their opinions. The simple fact was, once again, that he loved other people. That was his starting point, and his ending point as well. Love was both a cause and an effect of his openness, and in this love he abided by his own admonitions. He once described true love as that in which the beloved is left to his own freedom and solitude. We truly love someone, in other words, when we are capable of letting that person *be*, when we do not try to manipulate him, to mold him according to the image of what we think he should be. I think that the amazing array of diverse people who were attracted to Merton and considered it a privilege to be counted as his friends is emphatic testament to his ability to accept people on their own terms. If all of Merton's friends were to gather together in one place I would imagine that the results would be near chaotic. They probably would find it very difficult to get along with one another, and yet they all saw in him, in his magnanimous receptivity, something with which they could feel comfortable and at home. He was a pacifying and unifying influence because he was more concerned with understanding than arguing. Leaving it for the prosaic of the earth to mull over the clichés which explain what separates men, he took the high road of poetry and prophecy to discover those things which bind them together, which allow us to speak of Man rather than of men.

Finally, and above all else, Thomas Merton was a man of faith, and especially in this can he serve as a model for an age which is renowned for its wan, limp, and no doubt thoroughly frightened scepticism. There is nothing at all robust, nothing convincing, about our scepticism. Lincoln once observed of Americans that whereas they were not what you could call believers, neither did they have the fortitude definitely to disbelieve. The observation has wide applicability for

contemporary western society. We have the courage of neither a clear-cut yea or a clear-cut nay. But the energies which
we could be employing in making the assent of faith are not
going entirely unused. Short of making a commitment to real
faith, faith in a transcendent and loving God, we have created
ersatz faiths and upon these we dribble away our lives. As
was inevitable, we have substituted credulity for faith. We
claim that belief in a supreme being no longer holds any
meaning for us, and yet we seem to be quite comfortable in
the thought of "believing" in a Buick. Our faith, having lost
its vertical dimension, has spilled out upon the horizontal,
thinning and souring as it goes.

For Merton belief in God was not tangential; it lay at the
very core of life's meaning. There was a certain inevitability
to such belief, for to him, the discovery of God was a necessary adjunct to the discovery of oneself. God, as the Ground
of man's being, is encountered in man's descent into his
deepest self. If we do not know God, then, it is perhaps
because we really do not know ourselves. If any modern man
has put this theory to the test it was Merton. As a contemplative he was a miner of the soul. He knew well the darkness of
the lower depths and in that darkness he claimed to have
found the light. He confronted the meaningless and absurdity
head-on, and found them to be tentative realities. They told
only a part of man's story, and not the best part at that. The
best part was that man, for all his loneliness was not alone,
for all his fear was not ineluctably doomed, for all his
disgustingness was not irredeemably depraved. Man, born in
darkness, living in darkness, was in fact a child of the Light.
His salvation was to believe in the Light and, believing, to
seek after it incessantly. Thomas Merton showed how it
could be done.

THE CISTERCIAN FATHERS

NEW ENGLISH TRANSLATIONS

INTRODUCTION—NOTES—INDEXES

New English translations of the great Cistercian writers of the Twelfth Century, based on the recently established critical editions, with introductions, notes and indexes, prepared by competent scholars.

CISTERCIAN PUBLICATIONS
CONSORTIUM PRESS
Kalamazoo, Michigan
49001